The Meaning of
International Experience
for Schools

The Meaning of International Experience for Schools

ANGENE HOPKINS WILSON

PRAEGER

Westport, Connecticut
London

Library of Congress Cataloging-in-Publication Data

Wilson, Angene Hopkins.
    The meaning of international experience for schools / Angene
Hopkins Wilson.
        p.   cm.
    Includes bibliographical references and index.
    ISBN 0-275-94508-1 (alk. paper)
    1. International education—Case studies.   2. Intercultural
education—Case studies.   I. Title.
LC1090.W54   1993
370.19'6—dc20   92-38233

British Library Cataloguing in Publication Data is available.

Library of Congress Catalog Card Number: 92-38233
ISBN: 0-275-94508-1

First published in 1993

Praeger Publishers, 88 Post Road West, Westport, CT 06881
An imprint of Greenwood Publishing Group, Inc.

Printed in the United States of America

The paper used in this book complies with the
Permanent Paper Standard issued by the National
Information Standards Organization (Z39.48-1984).

10 9 8 7 6 5 4 3 2 1

Copyright Acknowledgment

The author and publisher are grateful to Beth Rambo for permission
to reprint an excerpt from her poem, ''Travelers,'' originally
published in *The Global Nomad Quarterly*, I, 1:6, 1992.

Contents

Acknowledgments

I could not have written this book without the willingness of many teachers and students to talk with me and let me sit in their classrooms. I cannot thank them enough. I thank especially Frankie Daniel, Mary Anne Flournoy, and Patricia Rice for their contributions.

I would not have written this book without my family. I thank my parents for giving me roots and wings, my husband for sharing love and equity for more than 30 years, my daughters for continuing to teach me, my extended family for also caring about and participating in international experience.

Introduction: From Lakewood to Liberia to Lexington

How this book came to be written may go back to 1946 when, as a seven-year-old, I wore flags representing countries of the new United Nations as a costume in a Fourth of July children's parade in Lakewood, Ohio.

I grew up in a family who considered human diversity and global connections both normal and positive. After World War II our family sent CARE packages to a family in Germany who sent us wooden puppets in return. When I was a teenager I had cousins who were living in New Zealand and Saudi Arabia. At a settlement house in downtown Cleveland, I taught swimming to children whose families had migrated from Appalachia and, after high school graduation, I spent three summers at a settlement house camp serving poor black and white children. There I worked with social workers from Germany who were participants in the Cleveland International Program (CIP), now the national Council of International Programs; a decade later, when I had my own family, CIP guests from Nigeria, Sudan, and Thailand lived with us in Columbus, Ohio.

My College of Wooster experience reaffirmed that I was a world-connected person, from my freshman roommate who had lived in Iran all her life to my summer study abroad in Paris. When President John F. Kennedy inaugurated the Peace Corps in 1961, the spring of my senior year, my husband-to-be and I stapled our applications together and sent them off to Washington. A little more than a year later we celebrated our first wedding anniversary in Liberia, a country the size of Ohio, in West Africa.

Teaching for two years in a bush boarding school run by black American Baptists was the most important experience of our lives. What came before the Peace Corps probably had something to do with why I joined. What came after followed because of what I learned in Liberia. White Americans, we were accepted as equal, no more and no less, by the Liberian and African-American colleagues with whom we worked and made lifelong friendships. We learned from them and also from Ma Becky, who told wonderful stories in Gola to small, wide-eyed boys on our living room porch. We learned from our students, too. We learned as we taught, finding books on African history in the Muslim bookstore in Monrovia and discovering the now world-famous writers Chinua Achebe and Wole Soyinka on a trip to Nigeria.

In those days I didn't know I was attaining what is now called a *global perspective*. I just knew that my international experience had made a profound difference in my life and that I felt the need to bring the world back home. For the next eight years I went to school (getting a masters in History and African Studies), taught in teacher training colleges in Sierra Leone and Fiji, and mothered two small daughters. After getting a doctorate in humanities education, I moved with my family to Lexington, Kentucky, where I have spent 18 years in teacher education, especially enjoying encouraging teachers to learn about the world. I have also been a volunteer with Youth for Understanding International Exchange for almost 10 years, hosting a Swedish son, sending two daughters on summer exchange experiences, and training other volunteers. In 1980 I led a six-week, Fulbright-funded study tour for teachers to Nigeria, and I have supervised student teachers in Colombia, Mexico, Ecuador, Costa Rica, England, Scotland, New Zealand, and Australia. The year 1991-92 was special because the son of Liberian friends from Peace Corps days lived with us and our friend Alfred from Peace Corps days also lived in Lexington while working on a graduate degree.

As I met people who had had experiences similar to mine and as I read the research on the impact of international experience on people, I began to ask others the question, "What has international experience meant to you?" For example, I asked that question of my older daughter Miatta, then a high school junior who had lived overseas for four years as a young Peace Corps child and who was at that point getting ready to be an exchange student in Switzerland. "You know there's someplace besides Lexington," she said. "I get mad when people think there are just huts and no tall buildings in Africa or when people assume you couldn't like an Iranian. The United States isn't all there is."

As I continued to read the research and talked to more people, I began to wonder as well how international experience can translate into an impact on the schools. This book tries to answer the question of the meaning of international experience for teachers, students, and schools by describing what some teachers and students who have had international experience do—and by recording what they think about what they do. The purpose for telling their stories is to demonstrate how internationally experienced persons act in schools and in some cases make a positive difference. The focus is on individual people and schools because I believe these stories of people and schools can offer models, mirrors, possibilities. They can elicit feelings of recognition (''Oh yes!'') and raise questions (''Now why is that?'').

Lakewood and Liberia influenced me, of course, but I must also admit the influence of Lexington. This book would have been written quite differently from the vantage point of, say, a gateway city on one of the U.S. coasts. One's personal glasses are colored by one's life experience, and that includes place. Lexington is not crowded with diversity; in fact, a one-time resident who had lived in Miami for 10 years returned several years ago to write a scathing article about his disappointment in the dull, homogeneous, prejudiced culture of central Kentucky. Perhaps the fact that his description is somewhat true sharpens the taste buds in anticipation of difference. Perhaps one yearns for the impact of international experience. However, Lexington is now becoming a cultural crossroads of north and south, urban and Appalachian, international and national. A new Toyota plant has had a particular impact on the area. In any case, besides being the location of several of the studies, Lexington is the place from which I set off to discover what other individuals and schools were doing.

It should be clear that this particular book is the product primarily of one person's research, one particular person with a particular life history. It has been said that we see what is behind our eyes. My eyes are those of an Anglo-American woman who grew up in a midwestern suburb and city, then went out to see and live in other parts of the world, and returned to be an ambassador for learning about and action in the world. There are other books to be written, for instance, by teachers who are themselves refugees or immigrants.

For me, the following African proverbs express an important truth about the concept of perspective. Even though I see what is behind my eyes, I can at least try on someone else's sunglasses or listen to another's voice.

> The world is like a Mask dancing; if you want to see it well you do not stand in one place.
>
> If you look only in one direction, your neck will be stiff.
>
> A person who has not visited other villages will think only his mother's cooking is sweet.

Also for me, the following conversation with my younger daughter, Cheryl, when she was seven, expresses an important truth about our common humanity. We are all on this earth together.

"Africa is different," Cheryl said.
"Yes?"
"They don't have telephones in Africa."
"Daddy had a telephone in his office in Sierra Leone," I said.
"The houses are different."
"Some are. Some aren't."
"The people are different."
"What about Alfred?" I asked. (Alfred of Africa, our boy-from-the-bush-made-good son, was visiting us that summer.)
Twinkle in her brown eyes.
Insight.
"Alfred's a man."

The concepts of perspective and common humanity are foundation stones for this book.

METHODOLOGY

The heart of this book is a collection of case studies. Besides the stories of teachers who have been short-term international sojourners and Peace Corps volunteers and the story of a refugee student and his teacher, three school studies—one of an affluent suburban elementary school, one of an impoverished rural middle school, and one of an inner city magnet high school program—look at the impact of international experience in a broader context. The first and second chapters look at the impact of international experience, problematically and theoretically. The last chapter offers specific suggestions for utilizing internationally experienced persons more fully.

For three reasons, a qualitative approach seemed most appropriate for my research. First, a qualitative approach fit with the philosophical assumptions that inform my answers to such questions as: how is truth defined? and what is the nature of educational inquiry? Truth is not "out there," but behind our eyes. Inquiry is the never-ending and uncertain process of interpreting the interpretations of others. Second, a qualitative approach fit with my perceptions of needed and useful research in global or international education. Descriptions of internationally experienced persons in schools could provide models showing how international experience can be connected to and utilized in classrooms. Finally, a qualitative approach fit with the topic of my research. Internationally experienced persons usually come to accept differences among peoples and cultures and recognize multiple perspectives and interpretations.

I completed a series of survey studies on the reentry of high school exchange students (cross-nationally) and on short-term international sojourner and returned Peace Corps volunteer teachers which are published elsewhere and listed in the bibliography, but I decided that case studies or "action snapshots," based mostly on classroom observation and interviews, would have the advantage of showing real people in the midst of the work of utilizing their international experience.

I considered myself a participant-observer, but I did more observing than participating. The teachers whose classes I describe in chapter 3 (Teachers with International Experience), in chapter 5 (Afghan Sixth Grader), and in chapter 8 (International Studies Academy) were observed over a school year for half or full days in repeated site visits. The teachers I describe in chapters 3 and 5 were observed approximately once a week; for chapter 8, I observed eight to ten classes each of the four teachers described in detail. Chapter 6 (A Little United Nations School) is based on two weeks of full-time immersion, and chapter 7 (International Student Visitors) is based on five days of immersion at two different times during one month. The returned Peace Corps volunteer vignettes in chapter 4 are the result of a minimum of observation of one class and an hour interview with each person.

I often engaged in informal conversation with students and teachers for chapters 3, 5, 6, and 8 and did many formal interviews. For chapters 3 and 5, I interviewed all the students and the teachers in the classes being observed. For chapter 6 (Little United Nations School), I interviewed all but one teacher in the school, plus 19 fourth, fifth, and sixth graders, and 13 parents. For chapter 7 (International Student Visitors), I interviewed the principal and the three teachers formally involved in the program twice and other teachers briefly, as well as the 60 students in the program. For chapter 8 (International Studies Academy), nine students were interviewed formally twice, and I also talked with most of them informally each time I visited. All the teachers and administrators were interviewed twice, and informal conversations were frequent. I also read a variety of school documents for the school studies, especially for the International Studies Academy.

Occasionally, I participated. For example, I took a "parental" turn at the Beech Valley bazaar, an "adviser" turn for the International Club at Washington by helping set up tables for their dinner, and a "teacher" turn by leading an activity on Nigeria for Angela's sixth grade class.

My major goal was to describe, but not mainly through my eyes. Although my perspective was inevitably important and I was the only researcher in these studies, the perspectives of the people in the situations were most important and informed my perspective. I wanted to understand their interpretations of what was happening, their meaning-making. The case studies of the Afghan sixth grader and of the middle school delineate multiple perspectives most clearly. The first shows the teacher's, Jimmy's, and the other students' and his family's perspectives, and the second describes the teachers', the middle school students', and the international students' perspectives. In all the school studies, students, teachers, and administrators were interviewed. In the elementary school study, parents were also interviewed. The perspectives of the people I observed are evident in the chapter titles. Titles were occasionally obvious, as in the third purpose of the Peace Corps, but they also evolved. For Jimmy, I wavered between "becoming American" and "making my country remembered." Both were important, but the latter seemed more important during that school year. The International Studies Academy title did not include "community" until that concept kept surfacing in conversations with some teachers and students and especially two administrators.

Preceding the case studies, I try to place international experience in the problematical arena of the school (chapter 1), and I explain how international experience has affected the individual (chapter 2). As I drew together the many research findings and considered how to illustrate the impact of international experience on students and teachers as individuals, I developed a graphic model which is still evolving. Some may wish to read the case studies first and then go back and read chapters 1 and 2.

In the last chapter, I try to be practical, though not prescriptive, about how teachers and students in schools, and higher education institutions and communities, can work together to utilize internationally experienced persons more fully.

No names used in this book are the actual names of the persons or the schools, although general place location is identified. The case studies or action snapshots are like freeze modeling in the sense that for the most part, they show people frozen in time. However, Angela and Michael continue to use their international experience in their teaching, Beech Valley is still such a "little United Nations" school—"naturally"—and the Ohio university continues its international student outreach to schools. The International Studies Academy magnet program has become more of an international education community, and, with the promotion of the associate principal who directed it to principal of the whole school, Washington High School is poised to become an international high school. Jimmy became a high school soccer star and has gone to college. The little girl who walked up the long hill home from Beech Valley went to Belgium as a high school exchange student and plans to major in comparative literature in college. International experience lives.

The Meaning of
International Experience
for Schools

Chapter 1

International Experience and Schools: The Context and the Problems

The world impinges on the school in many ways and sometimes seems to overwhelm it. The phrase "real world" implies that the school is another world, and yet that "real world" is there in the school.

First, there are students from so many different cultures attending schools. In a rural county in Kentucky, Japanese children whose fathers manage a plant there are entering a school system whose student body has previously been rather homogeneous. In an urban New York or Florida or California school, on the other hand, the born-in-America or native speaker of English child may be in the minority. About two-thirds of the 120,000 immigrant children who enrolled in New York City schools from 1988-92 were from 11 countries, including the Dominican Republic, 23,000; Jamaica, 18,000; Russia, 8,000; Guyana and China, 7,000 each; Haiti, 6,000; Trinidad, 4,800; Mexico, 4,200; Ecuador, 3,800; Colombia, 3,700; and Korea, 3,600 (*Christian Science Monitor*, 1992). In Hawaii, the multicultural mix of students is a reflection of a population that is 29% Caucasian, 23% Japanese, 17% Hawaiian, 11% Filipino, 5% Chinese, 2% Black, 1% Korean, 1% Samoan, .5% Puerto Rican, and 10.5% mixed or unknown (Zulich, 1989).

Second, there are global issues of so many kinds and of such complexity and seriousness, from hunger to environmental degradation. How can today's students be prepared to deal with competing needs such as jobs and environmental protection? How can they be prepared to communicate and learn across cultures on topics such as race relations or the role of women? How can they be prepared to recognize the difference between empowerment and dependency in an interdependent world and to understand how to act with respect for the dignity of each person?

These two ways in which the school is linked to the world—through people and through issues, and thus curriculum—may seem unconnected. Yet people—whether students, teachers, or administrators—are themselves resources, often untapped, for making the connection to the curriculum. Internationally experienced persons, including students and teachers who have traveled and/or lived in other countries, are particularly important resources. How can their international experience best be utilized? What do internationally experienced persons really have to offer?

This opening chapter looks at problems in connecting international experience to schools, while the second chapter looks at relevant research, trying to seek out and sort out possibilities for rationalizing and conceptualizing the utilization of international experience and its implications for schools.

THREE PROBLEMS

Three dichotomies become problems in considering how international experience can make a contribution to schools. One is the different way we tend to value international experience, depending on the situation of the person: an American winner of the Bundestag scholarship to be an exchange student in Germany for a year versus a Cambodian immigrant in an American high school. A second is the ambivalence of school culture toward international experiences and the ambivalent feelings of the internationally experienced persons themselves, both recent returnees and immigrants, about whether and how to share their experiences. The third is the tension between national and world citizenship and, in the United States, between the more traditional assimilation and multiculturalism.

Valuing International Experience?

Today travel, study abroad, and being an exchange student or teacher are usually seen as advantages for American young people and for teachers. Thomas Jefferson certainly thought otherwise. He wrote that "the consequences of foreign education are alarming to me as an American" (Tyack, 1967, 85). The founding fathers were interested in educating republicans and feared European contamination. The Georgia legislature even passed a law in 1785 disbarring its residents from civic office for as many years as they had studied abroad (if sent overseas under the age of 16) (Tyack, 1967, 85).

Certainly, in the twentieth century, there is "no doubt that international educational exchange has been wholeheartedly accepted in the United States" with appeals to pragmatism (peace is good for business) and idealism (an optimistic faith in person-to-person contact) (Speakman, 1966, 3), as well as concern for academic learning. In part, we have inherited the Grand Tour idea for eighteenth-century English gentlemen whose travel to France and Italy was a cultural, social, and political finishing school that would qualify them to take their places in the cosmopolitan upper class. There are undoubtedly modern-day students who have written letters home or called home to express sentiments similar to those in the following fictional letter which appeared in an English newspaper in 1753: "Pray, Sir, let me come home for I cannot find that one is a jot the better for seeing all these outlandish places and people" (Mead, 1914, 392). The fictitious letter writer and the modern-day casual tourist may be among those who travel "without taking thought" and thereby add not "a fraction of a cubit to their stature" (Abrams, 1965, 35). On the other hand, many internationally experienced people would probably concur with James Boswell, who wrote in 1764: "Nine months in this delicious country (Italy) have done more for me than all the sage lessons which books, or men formed by books, could have taught me" (Boswell, 1928, 3).

Educational travel and exchange have a long history. In fact, "travel," writes Leed in *The Mind of the Traveler* (1991, 15), "is a primary source of the 'new' in history." Roman young men went to study in Greece, for example, and folk tales in various cultures over the centuries have used the journey as a means to attain experience and wisdom. In the eighteenth century, Vattel, the Swiss father of international law, stated in *Le Droit des Gens* that the exchange of teachers is a common duty and service to humanity which nations should render to each other (Speakman, 1966).

In the second half of the twentieth century, international experience is usually seen as more than a finishing school, more than frosting on the educational cake, more than finding oneself. To the objectives of acquiring knowledge and developing self has been added the goal of promoting worldwide understanding. With the passage of legislation in 1946 initiating the Fulbright Program and in 1961 inaugurating the Peace Corps, cross-cultural education has also become accepted as a part of U.S. foreign policy. As Senator William Fulbright wrote, "Perhaps the greatest power of educational exchange is the power to convert nations into peoples and to translate ideologies into human aspirations" (Tuch, 1988, 31).

In their review of college and university study abroad programs, Goodwin and Nacht (1988) list ten educational and social purposes which they found during their research into several hundred programs: completing the finishing school and grand tour, broadening the intellectual elite, internationalizing the educated citizenry, fulfilling a distinctive institutional mission, exploring roots, mastering a foreign language, using the world as a laboratory, getting to know ourselves, learning from others, and improving international relations. They also listed more specific institutional purposes such as attracting students and creating interinstitutional linkages.

These goals did not spring into being in the last decade. More than 30 years ago, a California college president stated that study abroad was a necessity for American college students in order to develop far-seeing citizenship as insurance for survival. He also placed on the shoulders of students the responsibilities of being ambassadors for America around the world and being ambassadors to America after returning home (*Christian Science Monitor*, 1960, 9).

In the same decade, there was also concern about the education of teachers. In *The World as Teacher*, Taylor advocated a 25,000 member volunteer Student Corps which would place students in one-year community service teaching assignments in the United States and overseas. He wanted future teachers to have an opportunity to ''cross over, through their studies and their personal experience, to a culture different from the one in which they have been born and raised. Through entering other lives,'' he wrote, ''they begin to enter the world, and to provide themselves with something to compare themselves with, and by comparison to learn to look at mankind from a broader perspective'' (Taylor, 1969, ix).

Taylor recognized that the opportunity for incorporating international experience into the curriculum of high schools, colleges, and universities comes not only from Americans returning from overseas experience, but also from students of other nationalities coming to the United States. He described a program begun in Philadelphia in 1962 in which international students do short-term teaching about their cultures in public school classrooms.

In 1982 another college president, Ping of Ohio University, dealt with the issue of international students in a convocation address entitled ''The Search for International Community and Education for Interdependence.'' He began with a prescription found on an elementary classroom wall:

> We must study geography so that for us there is no foreign place.
> We must study humanity so that for us there is no foreign person. (Ping, 1982, 2)

After describing Ohio University's 28 agreements with overseas institutions and heavily international graduate student population from 86 countries, Ping offered proposals to deal with problems such as international students as an "underused resource for addressing knowledge and sensitivity to global issues" (1982, 9) and the lack of internationalization of the curriculum in the first two years of college.

Colleges and universities have usually worried more about the adaptation of foreign or international students to the United States and their sometimes problematic use as teaching assistants than about their possible contribution to public school and university international education. However, "international classroom" programs like the one Taylor described, which link international students and K–12 teachers in order to enrich elementary and secondary curricula, are now more common (Wilson, 1992). The state of Oregon has developed a program to enroll foreign students at in-state tuition in exchange for educational and cultural service (Van de Water, 1986, B4). The number of international students has grown from 34,000 in 1953 to nearly 400,000 in 1992 (plus 175,000 faculty and research scholars), so there are many potential contributors (Butler, 1992, 72).

If it has taken time to recognize foreign university students as resources for international learning, it has been equally or even more difficult to recognize elementary and secondary students from other cultures as contributors to the curriculum. This has been especially true for immigrant students. Instead of looking at international experience as a welcome advantage, schools have usually seen the different backgrounds of immigrants as a disadvantage and worked hard at assimilating them into American culture.

To return to the dichotomy as stated earlier, schools have often seen the experience of the Bundestag scholarship winner and the experience of the Cambodian refugee very differently: "What a wonderful opportunity to learn German well!" versus "I can't understand her at all!" Miller, writing about a similar point of view in England toward the language of immigrant students, states:

> Whereas learning a foreign language and even one or two dead ones as well has always been the sine qua non of a "good" education, and whereas a child who picks up fluent French and Italian, say, because her father has been posted abroad, is likely to be thought fortunate, at an advantage, even "finished," a child with two or three non-European languages in some of which he may be literate, could be regarded as quite literally languageless when he arrives in an English school where "not a word of English" can often imply "not a word. . . ."
>
> It is a characteristic irony that while the learning of languages can be an expensive business, nearly all those people in the world who grow up or become bilingual do so because their mother tongue or dialect has associations with poverty which make it likely to be thought inappropriate for education and some kinds of employment. (Miller, 1983, 5 and 8)

King, looking at the implications of Britain's Mother Tongue Project for American education, agrees:

> In the past in British and American schools, children speaking a language other than English were seen not as possessing a set of valuable skills but as struggling against an impediment that needed to be eradicated before they could successfully acquire the English language and thus take advantage of the learning opportunities available in society. (King, 1984, 4)

One way to make a conscious switch from the deficit model is to rephrase problems facing immigrant youth. Instead of English language deficiencies, there is a lack of appreciation of the languages of immigrant children. Instead of immigrant children's difficulty in socializing with local children, there is a difficulty of local children socializing with immigrant children. Instead of a lack of relevant schooling in the native country, there is a lack of relevant curriculum in the local school for the previous schooling experience of immigrant children. Instead of difficulty of immigrant children understanding American values, there is difficulty in understanding and appreciating values of the immigrant culture. Such rephrasing is important because "the major consequence of possessing the power to label persons as deviants or problems is that one can define the problem in a way that requires others to make the adjustment" (Agbayani, 1979, 3 and 4).

Two theories utilized to explain immigrant behavior in schools also need to be reconsidered. One focuses on cultural differences and assumes that educational problems arise because of a mismatch between the culture of the students and the culture of the school. A second theory emphasizes the structural relationship between groups of people and assumes low achievement is a consequence of the American system of social stratification. Research on Punjabi immigrants in California contradicts both theories. Immigrant students can deal constructively with discontinuities between the home and school setting and, despite discrimination, immigrant students can do well in school (Gibson, 1983).

Restating the problem and reconsidering the theories are not enough, however. How do the bilingualism or multilingualism and, more broadly, the international experience of the immigrant children receive not only recognition of the relevance for their own learning but also for that of young natives of the culture in which the immigrant children find themselves? Such recognition probably requires a view of school as a place in which the immigrants are actors who have some control, some role, rather than subjects who are acted on by the school (Weiss, 1982, xv). Indeed, "a pupil's ethnic background, far from implying a vacuum or emptiness in his previous or nonschool experiences, may indicate a wealth of resources which the teacher might know and draw upon" (Moore, 1976, 252).

Further, the problem needs to be defined not as ethnicity but as ethnic borders. "In most cases, it has become clear that the differences between people are only incidentally a problem; the differences between people are as much a resource for mutual exploration and celebration as they are a resource for conflict" (McDermott and Gospedinoff, 1981, 216).

Finally, we need to look for commonalities in the experiences of internationally experienced persons, be they immigrants or sojourners. Kim (1989) argues for a theoretical integration of the adaptation process to include all cultural strangers, and thus both immigrants and sojourners. Recognizing the differences—immigrants must depend on the host environment and go through more extensive adaptation, while sojourners depend less on the host environment and have a relatively short stay—Kim nevertheless suggests that there are commonalities in intercultural adaptation worth exploring.

One commonality immigrant students have with returning exchange students is that neither group's experiences are recognized as relevant to the curriculum. A high school junior talked about her opportunities to share a summer experience in Japan.

> In French class we talk about issues and I say "In Japan this happened or in Japan this is the case." I asked the World Civ teacher if he wanted me to speak to his class about Japan and he said "When are you going?" When I said I went last summer, he said they had already studied Japan for this year. But next year I'm taking International Relations.

In a study of high school exchange students who had returned from a summer in Japan, only 50% of the students had talked with teachers more than three times about their experiences after being back for about two months. Making a special presentation to a class about the Japan experience was something 21% of the students had done more than three times, but 32% of the students had never made a special presentation (Wilson, 1985).

The exchange student, the immigrant student, the returned Peace Corps volunteer teacher have much to offer. If the experience is valued, why is it often not shared?

Ambivalence of School Culture and of the Internationally Experienced

The school culture is often ambivalent about internationally experienced persons, and sometimes students who are immigrants and returnees are ambivalent about whether and how to share their experiences. Conformist teenage culture is one barrier to more sharing of the international experience by both exchange student returnees and immigrant students. Students do not want to be seen as "weird experts." It may be more acceptable, even for elementary students, to have gone to Disney World than to have come from Afghanistan or returned from Argentina. The internationally experienced student may decide it is easier, more sensible to fit in, adapt, or revert.

Another barrier may be the teacher. At the high school level, the pressure to "cover" the subject in the book in chronological order and the tradition of teacher-directed lecture-discussions discourage the use of guests, especially at "inappropriate" times. The teacher may also feel threatened by the knowledge of the cross-culturally experienced student, since university preparation, experience, and the economic status of teachers militate against most teachers in most schools having had firsthand experience of another culture. "One study of global education among elementary teachers in Missouri found that the problem was not so much one of getting teachers to endorse the need for global education, as it was their lack of academic preparation for the task, their feelings of being pressured by competing demands on classroom time, and the minimum opportunities they had had to experience other cultures" (Wright and Van Decar cited in Grossman, 1992).

For students, a third barrier is the institutional culture of the school which is an asymmetrical situation in terms of power. Students need an invitation to speak to a class, often even one in which they are enrolled, and school permission to speak to an elementary class. The institutional culture of the school may seem unwelcoming to internationally experienced adults as well. In a survey of social studies teachers who are returned Peace Corps volunteers, 50% agreed somewhat with the statement "My school isn't receptive and people on the staff aren't interested" and 22% agreed somewhat with the statement "I don't ever talk about the Peace Corps because people here wouldn't understand" (Wilson, 1986b). The problem with the second statement is that it can be interpreted as reflecting the occasional arrogance of internationally experienced persons who, from the point of view of the untraveled, flaunt their travel and "superior" understanding. The internationally experienced person understands well the lament of the ancient Chinese poem which begins, "How shall I talk of the sea to the frog who has never left his pond?"

While study abroad is well accepted on college campuses, returnees face frustrations similar to those of high school returnees. An interview study of returnees on a university campus and a small liberal arts college campus revealed that about two-thirds of the students had talked to professors about their experiences and one-third had talked about their experiences in class discussions. About one-quarter had spoken to an adult group.

A woman who had spent her junior year in Denmark said:

I live in the international dorm and some of us eat dinner together once a

week, but that isn't enough. I've talked with my German prof and I got a
very positive response from my professor in an education course. I'd like
to talk to an adult group or to elementary or secondary students but no one
has invited me. (Wilson, n.d.)

The fact is that reentry, as it is called, is not easy for returnees. From a
communication perspective, for both the internationally experienced
American and the immigrant to the United States, learning to live in
another culture demands that the person "modify the original meaning
structure and internalized rules of interaction to learn a new complex of
verbal and nonverbal communication patterns" (Martin, 1986, 4). For
persons returning to their own cultures, there is another adaptation.
When the returnee who has learned the new communication patterns
comes home with a changed meaning structure and encounters old
symbols and rules, confusion in interacting with friends and family may
result. (The returnee from a so-called third world country may look at
the bounty and materialism of the supermarket—an old symbol—with a
different perspective, for example.) But through communication with
family and friends, returnees usually begin to understand the changes
wrought by cross-cultural experience and to integrate those changes into
their future lives.

Immigrants and exchange students face even greater challenges in
communicating. In addition, for some immigrants, residence in their
own cultural communities and an almost ascribed lower socioeconomic
class can also be barriers to interaction with so-called mainstream
students.

So the school may be ambivalent, and the internationally experienced
student or teacher may be ambivalent. The result may be that the
resources for learning about the world are not utilized.

For What Purpose?

Why should schools be interested in utilizing internationally
experienced students and teachers? Isn't it better for the immigrant
student or the exchange student or teacher returnee to "just adjust"?
Schools may accept some "show and tell," but the message following
that brief sharing is often "fit in." That view fits with the concept of
traditional assimilation represented by the image of the melting pot.

The concept of cultural pluralism, on the other hand, represented by
the image of a salad bowl, offers more possibilities for the internationally
experienced. The salad bowl has room for differences, even differences
that last. As a cherry tomato will not change into a cauliflower floret, so
the young Muslim woman whose parents came from Jordan will not
necessarily become a typical suburban teenager in dress or beliefs. A
Mexican-American man, talking about a multiethnic high school in

California said, ''You have lettuce, you have tomatoes, you have cukes, you have onions, whatever. You chop 'em up and throw 'em into a bowl. You toss it and it's very good; it tastes very good together, but each one still has its distinct taste to it'' (Peskin, 1991, 215).

There are other images. A Sicilian-American man, talking about the same high school, said: ''It's like you're making a minestrone soup. You put a lot of different ingredients in it and you get something unique from it. You don't taste carrots and you don't taste beef and you don't taste onions. You taste it all. I think that's what is happening here today. . . . It goes beyond their own ethnic identity'' (Peskin, 1991, 216). Writes Reed (1988, 159): ''The world has been arriving at these shores for at least ten thousand years from Europe, Africa, and Asia. In the late nineteenth and early twentieth centuries, large numbers of Europeans arrived, adding their cultures to those of the European, African, and Asian settlers who were already here, and recently millions have been entering the country from South America and the Caribbean, making the . . . bouillabaisse richer and thicker.''

However, whether using salad bowl, minestrone, bouillabaisse, or quilt or rainbow or another metaphor, even those who see pluralism as a promising and necessary approach have asked: ''What nexus can be forged between individual rights and group solidarity, between universalistic principles and particularistic needs?'' And they have noted that the ''greater problem in moving toward pluralistic integration may come in rediscovering what the participants in our kaleidoscopic culture have in common'' (Higham, 1974, 73). The poignant cry of Rodney King ''Can we all get along?'' (*Time* cover, May 11, 1992), during the spring 1992 Los Angeles riots, is indicative of a pervasive concern for building community. Can ideals of justice and tolerance, even love and peace, become a universally accepted ''house'' salad dressing?

Patrick (1986) suggests that Higham's concept of pluralistic integration—seeing both integration and ethnic cohesion as goals which different individuals will accept in different degrees—is more congruent with social reality and more compatible with education for citizenship in the United States than monolithic integration or ethnocentric pluralism. Pluralistic integration is a middle ground between those who wish to focus mainly on celebrating individual ethnic groups and those who believe ''multiculturalism'' is ''disuniting America'' and advocate a return to a traditional canon. Barber (1992), also seeking middle ground, points out the excesses of both left and right in the current debate and proposes a civic education rooted in service learning in the community. To Barber, American identity is based not on culture but on the principle of rights, and the American story continues to be constructed as Americans continue to hope and to struggle. West, an African American looking for middle ground, writes that ''the most valuable sources for

help, hope and power consist of ourselves and our common history"
and that "we must focus our attention on the public square—the
common good that undergirds our national and global destinies," invest
in infrastructure and people, and generate new leadership (1992, 26).

But the debate is not confined to goals and content for the education of
the multiethnic population of American schools. Young people in many
nations are part of multicultural populations (in some cases nations
which are currently torn by ethnic strife) and are living in a world "in
which our well-being increasingly depends on how we get on with each
other" (Kleinjans, 1974, 20). Evidence of the multiculturalism of
populations is the fact that in one recent year high school exchange
students going from central Kentucky included an Asian Indian American and students coming to Kentucky included a German of Ethiopian
parentage and a Dutch student of Indonesian and Guyanese parentage.

The discussion of pluralism is an issue not only within the nation-
state. Many also wonder how to reconcile loyalty to an ethnic group
and/or a nation and loyalty to the larger world.

> Where on the spectrum of exclusivity–tolerance should a person stand?
> How can a person have deep beliefs which he holds firmly without becom-
> ing dogmatic, bigoted, and divisive? But also, how can he develop a sense of
> tolerance toward other cultures, other sets of priorities and values without
> becoming completely relativistic or apathetic? (Kleinjans, 1974, 25)

Kleinjans saw the struggle toward an ethical basis for internationalism
as a very important task for the future and did not assume that only
Western values would contribute to that ethical basis.

In fact, American schools can no longer assume that only students
with Western values come to school. Further, learning about other
cultures is truly complicated. It involves more than appreciating flower-
arranging or eating sushi for the first time, or alternatively, appreciating
square dancing or eating grits. It involves a consideration of other values
and an acknowledgment of cultural relativity, though not necessarily
the acceptance of other values for oneself. It involves dealing with real
people from other cultures, appreciating the cultural context but getting
to know the individual. For example, a lesson on Buddhism from a Stan-
ford Program on International and Cross-cultural Education (SPICE)
unit on religion and cultural transmission in Japan includes profiles of
three different Buddhist leaders and their beliefs and values (Mukai,
1992). However much a person may be like other persons because of
ethnicity, there are still ways in which he or she is like all other persons,
regardless of ethnicity, and there are still ways in which a particular
person is like no other person (Harrington, 1975).

Internationally experienced students and teachers usually understand that learning about other cultures is complicated. High school exchange students or college international students coming here from more group-oriented societies find it difficult to deal with this more individualistic society. Immigrant schoolchildren coming here from societies with different ideas about parent-child relationships or male-female roles may find it hard to decide whether to follow the family/original cultural values or the new American values. For task- and time-oriented Americans who return from living in another culture with less emphasis on both, the question may be how to temper getting things done with a concern for interpersonal relationships.

One way to try to leap over the dichotomy of loyalty to nation or culture versus appreciation of the wider world may be to accept that the United States, like all other countries, is part of an increasingly interconnected world system. With the declining hegemony of Western civilization and the movement toward a multipolar rather than a bipolar world, American society will become more deeply integrated into the world system. So it really isn't a case of competing loyalties. We have no choice but to be concerned about the world we live in, as well as our own nation or cultural group.

As Mikhail Gorbachev said to longtime Soviet expert George Kennan in 1987: "We in our country believe that a man may be a friend of another country and remain, at the same time, a loyal and devoted citizen of his own; and that is the way we view you" (Kennan, 1989, 351). In Kennan's view, "To understand things beyond one's original cultural horizon is only to add them, in a sense, to what one already is. To do this does not mean that what one already is becomes discarded" (1989, 363).

However, one group of Americans, who lived overseas as children (called absentee Americans or third culture kids or global nomads), have not added to their citizenship because they have never felt like Americans. Writes one: "I am a citizen of Spaceship Earth" (Smith, 1991, 79). Writes another: "I feel as though I'm a member of a much larger community than one nation. Now it has come into vogue to talk about the 'global village' that I feel I've been a member of for most of my life" (Smith, 1991, 57). Such Americans and children of other national origins who grow up in the United States may speak for the future.

Anderson (1982) stated more than a decade ago that "Why should American education be globalized?" is a nonsensical question. In a chapter entitled "A Rationale for Global Education" in *Global Education: From Thought to Action* (Tye, 1990) and in the introduction to *Global Education: A Study of School Change* (Tye and Tye, 1992), Anderson again makes the point that since education mirrors society and we live in a global society, education has to deal with that world. Anderson explains how the process of globalization, under way since at least 1492, has accelerated rapidly over the past 20 years in the economy, in politics, in demography, and in culture. Kentucky Fried Chicken in China, the involvement of Kentucky state government in bringing Toyota to the Bluegrass, the presence of Asian Indian professors and Mexican migrant workers, and world beat music on the radio are evidence for one state.

Recognition of the importance of the global environment is also basic to the idea of a world system. The population of the whole world suffers if tropical rainforests, the most biologically diverse areas on earth, are destroyed. Yet care for the environment has to be balanced with care for people—what is being called sustainable development—and an awareness of the perspectives of others, who might consider our biotechnology to be bio-imperialism. The need to conserve scarce water resources and to eliminate acid rain are examples of environmental problems that have no borders. Some other problems without borders, problems that North, South, East, and West increasingly share, include AIDS, preparedness for natural disasters, homelessness, human rights, teenage pregnancy, and ethnic tensions (Korten, 1990). An understanding of the world as a global system and of our therefore global responsibility does not negate the rich variety and conflicting values of different cultures. It does offer a framework for considering universal values, such as justice, to which most persons might subscribe.

THE BASIC QUESTIONS

So can schools see the validity of the international experiences of the American exchange student or returned Peace Corps volunteer teacher *and* the "third world" refugee, first generation immigrant? Can schools be welcoming to internationally experienced persons *and* can such persons figure out appropriate ways to contribute? Can schools deal with the wonder of cultural variety *and* common global concerns? Finally, can schools, with help from the internationally experienced persons in their midst, teach about both cultural variety and global issues?

Further questions about these internationally experienced persons may be raised. Again and most basic, what can they really offer? Do those teachers and students with international experience know how to contend with clashing cultural values in themselves, in others? Because they know more than one culture, can they see worth in more than one culture? Can they see prejudices against others as well as against themselves? Can they see hunger and homelessness, celebration and creativity in places other than their own backyard? Are they able to build on their international experience to attain a global perspective and then help others see the bigger picture, too? In sum, have they reflected on their international experience, thought about what it means? Finally, what is the impact of international experience on students and teachers and what does and could that impact have to do with education in schools?

Chapter 2

The Impact of International Experience

Eleanor Roosevelt considered her travels with Marie Souvestre, the head of Allenswood School in London where she spent three years, "one of the most momentous things that happened in my education . . . I really marvel now at myself—confidence and independence, for I was totally without fear in this new phase of my life," she wrote of her travels in Europe as a teenager (Cook, 1992, 115).

"My mind has to create things and, when they are completed, go on to another venture. But some ventures refuse to be over. I never sleep one night without dreaming of Arabia," wrote Ronald Blythe in *Akenfield* (1969).

Such reflection about the meaning of international experience is not uncommon and has support in research. The following review of research includes studies focusing on high school exchange students, college study abroad students, Peace Corps volunteers, teachers and professors, and absentee (or third culture or global nomad) Americans. The net is purposefully cast broadly, but does not deal with all of the numerous possible impacts of international experience. Historically, for instance, a case can be made for the importance of experience in the American Revolution to members of the French aristocracy and thus a case for American values as a cause of the French Revolution (Schama, 1989). This review, however, is restricted to outcomes relevant to formal education.

One way to visualize the impact of international experience as described in the research is shown in Figure 1. Internationally experienced persons begin to gain a global perspective (substantive knowledge and perceptual understanding) and develop self and relationships (personal growth and interpersonal connections). In turn, that global perspective and personal and interpersonal development can be passed on to the school as internationally experienced teachers and students play the role of cultural mediator.

To illustrate, consider Donna who did her student teaching in England. She gained substantive knowledge about British primary schools through her teaching in a small village school and about British history through her visits to nearby London. She gained perceptual understanding through, among other experiences, interaction with British youngsters who taught her that the words ''rubber'' and ''boot'' could be used in more than one way. Personally, she became more self-confident and independent after traveling across the Atlantic and on trains and the ''tube''

Figure 1
The Impact of an International Experience

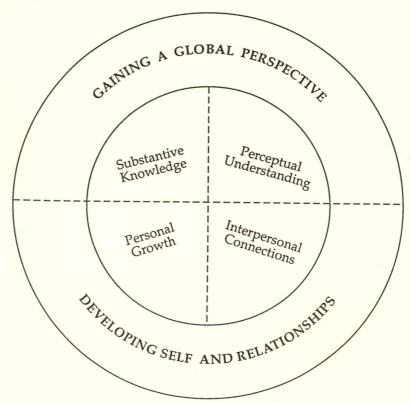

by herself. After she returned, several British friends visited her on their holiday. During the several years that she has been teaching in Kentucky she has used many materials and ideas brought back from England, and has recently asked to help with the mandated reform for ungraded primary classes because of her British experience.

GAINING A GLOBAL PERSPECTIVE: SUBSTANTIVE KNOWLEDGE

Substantive knowledge can be very specific: learning a second language—Thai or Arabic—or learning about the art of Michelangelo, the history of Sudanic empires in West Africa, the flora and fauna of Costa Rica, the trading patterns of Australia. Substantive knowledge is similar to intellectual development or cognition in the model proposed by Kauffmann, Martin, and Weaver (1992) in their book on college-level study abroad programs. They include learning a language, gaining a new perspective on a major, and increasing knowledge in general studies as aspects of intellectual development.

Borrowing from Case's (1991) definition of a substantive dimension of the global perspective, substantive knowledge also includes global issues, such as national and international security and choices for the future on those issues. Case combines the frameworks of Kniep (1986) and Hanvey (1976) to describe five elements of the substantive dimension: universal and cultural values and practices, global interconnections, present concerns and conditions, origins and past patterns, and alternatives and future directions.

Knowledge is basic to education, both learning and teaching. Henry has pointed out the connection between role involvement and knowledge. He maintained that as knowledge increases in any culture, ignorance tends to increase for individuals. Since knowledge, according to Henry, is related to role performance or involvement, it follows that teachers who have no role involvement in the subject matter they teach cannot be said to really have knowledge of that subject matter. "For example," wrote Henry, "anthropologists would not ordinarily tend to make mistakes about the geography of areas on which they specialize, for their role performance enforces knowledge of those areas; but elementary teachers who have never been to Europe or worked in a travel agency or an importing or exporting company might have but the haziest notions of the geography of Europe." Henry continues:

A draftsman or a surveyor would be expected to be able to calculate a periphery rapidly and correctly, for his role performance requires this. But a teacher is role involved only in teaching; he knows about peripheries only at second hand, and therefore is likely to make mistakes in calculating them. In

stark contrast with contemporary industrial societies, teachers in all
nonliterate cultures are role involved in what they teach; archery is taught to
children by accomplished hunters, agriculture by husbandsmen, religion by
men and women who practice what they preach. (Henry, 1976, 153)

Role involvement in the form of international experience can provide
teachers with knowledge, as is evident in several studies. In a study of
the impact of high school social studies teachers' backgrounds on the
implementation of global education curricula, Thorpe (1988) found statistically significant associations between travel abroad (the number of
countries a teacher had visited) and respondents' knowledge self-
ratings. Wieber (1982) discovered that the number of countries a teacher
had visited had a statistically significant association with a teacher's performance on a global knowledge assessment. In a survey study, Wilson
(1984) described gains in knowledge reported by teachers who were
short-term travelers. The teachers wrote that they taught with more
accuracy, authority, creativity, enthusiasm, and understanding about
the places they had visited. In another study of teachers who participated in summer study tours, Gilliom (n.d.) found that teachers learned
most about the history, geography, and culture of the countries
visited. They reported that they taught more accurately and creatively
and with more credibility about the countries they visited. For example,
one noted "the ability to give eyewitness accounts to my students." Tye
and Tye hypothesize, from their global education project research in
southern California, that "teachers [later they include principals] who
have lived overseas, those who begin following world news early in life,
and those whose parents discussed current events with them while they
were growing up would be more apt to become involved in global
education" (1992, 59). They also provide concrete examples, as do
Gilliom's teachers, of how the results of international travel, such as
slides and specially developed units, are used in teaching.

For high school students, the AFS International/Intercultural Programs'
Impact Study offers important support for the knowledge outcome of
international experience. In this exchange organization's study of 2,500
secondary school students from many nations, characteristics and definitions of personal growth from an intercultural homestay, developed
from interviews and written solicitation from returnees, were then
tested through a questionnaire employing a self-rating technique. Of the
17 variables in the study, the following 4 were found to be strongly associated with the AFS homestay:

Awareness and Appreciation of Host Country and Culture: Considerable knowl-
    edge of the people and culture of my host country, and an understand-
    ing of that country's role in world affairs.

Foreign Language Appreciation and Ability: Ability to communicate with people in a second language and thus to take advantage of opportunities and alternatives resulting from bi-lingualism.

Understanding Other Cultures: Interest in learning about other peoples and culture; ability to accept and appreciate their differences.

International Awareness: An understanding that the world is one community; a capacity to empathize with people in other countries; an appreciation of the common needs and concerns of people of different cultures. (Hansel, 1983, 7)

Several exchange student comments are illustrative:

Nothing can replace the feeling I had when, after returning, I went to my Spanish class. My teacher started crying because she was so proud that I could speak Spanish fluently. (Grove & Hansel, 1982, 19)

My AFS experience gave me a heightened awareness of global problems—an awareness much greater than that generated by the fear of surprise current events tests in high school. (AFS statement, n.d., 5)

Hansel makes the important point in the AFS Final Report that exchange students gained a different kind of knowledge than the ordinary tourist/traveler. "While many of the students may have seen famous sights in their host country, none mentioned this as an outcome of their experience" (1986, 30). Instead they mentioned the outcomes, such as language learning and learning about world affairs, described above.

Another earlier study, with 200 subjects and 200 controls, measured the effects of a 10-month AFS program on Turkish teenagers, confirming that gains in knowledge are not limited to American teens. Adapting and using a world-mindedness scale, Kagiticibasi (1978) found that AFS students were more likely to increase in world-mindedness than students who had not had the experience abroad.

Knowledge of international affairs and of the host country are given high marks as outcomes of study abroad programs, too, according to findings from the Study Abroad Evaluation Project, which studied Americans at institutions in the United Kingdom, France, Germany, and Sweden. Study abroad returnees showed a significantly greater interest in international affairs. Their knowledge about their host country increased dramatically, especially knowledge of the system of postsecondary education, cultural life, customs and traditions, social structure, and dominant social issues (Carlson and others, 1990, 1991). A smaller study on reentry adjustment states that 84% of the returnees reported a "clear, long-lasting change of their perceptions on global issues (Uehara, 1986, 433). More than 75% of Brigham Young University study abroad students reported that the semester abroad had had con-

siderable impact on their interest in world affairs and on their understanding of cultural differences in the world (Baker, 1983).

The Study Abroad Evaluation Project shows that students make significant gains in language proficiency (Carlson and others, 1990, 1991).
The Brigham Young University study also reports results relating particularly to foreign language appreciation: study abroad students
showed a greater enrollment in foreign language than the control
students not only before study abroad but also afterwards (Baker, 1983).

In *A Profile of the U.S. Student Abroad*, self-assessment of the impact of
the international experience revealed an increased interest in international events. Although questions about knowledge of host country
or foreign language appreciation were not on this questionnaire, it is
relevant that "foreign language" and "improve knowledge of country"
were the most important goals for the U.S. student abroad, following
"add new dimension to schooling" which was most often ranked first.
The profile also shows increased political awareness by study abroad
students (Koester, 1985).

Finally, a study describing self-reported outcomes of student teaching
in the United Kingdom included acquisition of content knowledge, form
the metric system to British history. The percentage (65%) of student
teachers indicating learning in that category was sixth out of nine, but
selection and creation of curricular materials, the first (96%), and choice
and use of various instructional activities, fifth (79%), also seem related to
content knowledge (Mahan and Stachowski, 1985).

GAINING A GLOBAL PERSPECTIVE:
PERCEPTUAL UNDERSTANDING

International experience clearly contributes to a gain in the perceptual
understanding of an individual. In his perceptual dimension of a global
perspective, Case (1991) lists open-mindedness (drawing on Hanvey's
[1976] perspective consciousness—the recognition that one has a worldview not universally shared), anticipation of complexity, resistance to
stereotyping, inclination to empathize, and non-chauvinism. The perceptual understanding category presented here also includes Brislin's
notion of complexity of thinking, "the ability to consider many different
points of view when making decisions" (1981, 2); the AFS characteristic
of critical thinking, "an inclination to be discriminating and skeptical of
stereotypes and a tendency not to accept things as they appear on the
surface" (n.d.); and the concepts of reflective thinking and reflection in
action (Vall and Tennison, 1991-92).

Findings in a number of studies relate to perceptual understanding. In
a study of German and American Youth for Understanding Exchange
student returnees, for example, approximately 85% of all respondents

indicated that the exchange experience caused an attitudinal change which led them to begin to individualize people, rather than stereotype them by nationality (Bachner and Zeutschel, 1990). Hoffman and Zak (1969) earlier reported a favorable change in attitude toward another nationality, related to high interpersonal contact. Occasional anecdotal evidence is also revealing. For example, one teacher responding to Gilliom's questionnaire (n.d.) noted that after the study tour to Kenya she was no longer shy of adults with black skin and another admitted confronting her own racism when she realized she expected a white hotel manager, because "she had accepted that black people could not manage such places on their own with such skill."

All AFS respondents in the Impact Study showed some increase in the characteristic of critical thinking, with those year and short program students who had not previously been abroad showing a significantly greater increase than the comparison group of respondents who had never been abroad. A comment from an American female student who lived in Jordan illustrates:

> I've found that I have become more closed-minded due to my AFS experi-
> ence. I believe, however, that this is not necessarily bad because my total
> open-mindedness was out of my ignorance of so many subjects. Although
> I'm closed-minded about some things, I still analyze and try to understand
> why or how something is the way it is. Occasionally, I can't accept the idea
> or the way the people think and in that way I am closed-minded. (Grove
> and Hansel, 1983, 12)

As for reflective thinking, Stewart's (1976) study of New Zealand AFS students, which included use of a values scale, showed that AFS students became more theoretical over the year than did the control students. In a study of the Goshen College study and service abroad program, Kauffmann (1982) found increased interest in reflective thought and tolerance for ambiguity. One year later, that increase persisted. In a recent study of American student teachers in Britain, the researchers found that, because of the differences between American and British school systems, the student teachers developed reflective thinking about teaching and incorporated that reflective thinking into their teaching (Vall and Tennison, 1991-92).

DEVELOPING SELF AND RELATIONSHIPS: PERSONAL GROWTH

Substantive knowledge and perceptual understanding overlap to some degree as aspects of gaining a global perspective. For example, Hanvey's dimension of cross-cultural awareness and the AFS characteristic of international awareness require both substantive knowledge about the cultural practices of a country's inhabitants and the perceptual understanding to imagine the practice from the "native" point of view.

So, too, the development of self and relationships overlaps with the gaining of a global perspective. Illustrating that overlapping, Kauffmann, Martin, and Weaver (1992) propose a model for understanding the study abroad international experience in which growth in cognition goes hand in hand with growth in other aspects of personality as the student interacts with a new environment. In study abroad the student moves from equilibrium through disequilibrium toward a new equilibrium.

Besides cognition, their developmental "education as change" model suggests five other variables which mediate the interaction of the student and the environment of the international experience: autonomy, belonging, values, vocation, and worldview. "Autonomy" in their model is related to the changes in self-confidence and feelings of independence noted by many returnees from international experience and included in Figure 1 here as part of personal growth. Expanding "values" options, exploring what one's life "vocation" is to be, and developing a "worldview" or unifying perception are related to perceptual understanding and personal growth. "Belonging" in their model is related to building connections and to community—dealt with in Figure 1 here as part of interpersonal connections.

Peter Adler's concept of a transitional experience, which describes what happens to the person undergoing an international experience, is also helpful. He suggests that

> specific psychological, social, and cultural dynamics occur when new cultures are encountered and these behavioral dynamics are, in large part, a function of perceptions of similarities and differences as well as changed emotional states. The model of the transitional experience also implies that a successful cross-cultural experience should result in the movement of personality and identity to new consciousness of values, attitudes, and understandings. (1975, 15)

Adler explains that the transitional experience begins with an encounter with self. His model begins at contact with the other culture and moves to disintegration (depression and withdrawal may result from impact of cultural differences), then to reintegration (differences are rejected by a person who is angry, frustrated, rebelling, but assertive), then to autonomy (when differences and similarities are legitimized and one becomes confident and empathic), and finally to independence (when differences and similarities are valued, significant, and understood and the person exercises choice and responsibility).

Adler's final stage, independence, and related characteristics such as autonomy (listed as one of the "education as change" variables) and self-confidence are mentioned in numerous studies. For instance, the AFS Impact Study definition for Independence: Responsibility for Self reads: "Ability to exercise self-control and to be self-directed; capacity to avoid beng a conformist and to resist peer pressure" (Hansel, 1983, 7). Again, exchange students with no previous travel experience showed a significantly greater change than the comparison group. Somewhat confusing is the result that short program students were much more likely to report great changes in this area than both year and untraveled comparison students. It could be that short program students were not as independent as year students before they went. In another study, Kagiticibasi (1978) found partial support for the hypothesis that AFS students would show a greater increase in internal control, which can be related to independence. Stitsworth (1988), who used the California Psychological Inventory with 4-H exchange students spending a month in Japan, as well as controls, found that the overseas group increased in independence.

High school and college students in *A Profile of the U.S. Student Abroad* listed increased self-confidence as an outcome of experience abroad, so increase in that characteristic does not seem to be uniquely associated with the homestay abroad experience. In studies of college students, Nash (1976) found that study abroad students to France increased in their autonomy, and Baker (1983) reported that the experience had a positive impact on students' self-confidence. In a study of University of Göttingen program participants, the largest number of responses to a question about personal maturation involved "growth in independence, self-reliance, and ability to make decisions on one's own" (Billigmeier and Forman, 1975 in Sell, 1983, 134).

In recent research on the Harlaxton College (England) study abroad program, students reported the greatest overall area of change on personal growth dimensions, including increased self-confidence and independence (Thomlison, 1991). Growth in self-confidence was also an outcome of student teaching in England (Vall and Tennison, 1991-92). Finally, results of an evaluation of the Consortium for Overseas Student Teaching (at the time most students taught in Latin American countries) showed growth in acceptance of self and others, general maturity, acceptance of responsibility, and especially independence (McKiernan, 1980). However, the expectation that study abroad would result in increased levels of self-confidence was not supported in the Study Abroad Evaluation Project (Carlson and others, 1990).

Peace Corps studies report independence and related characteristics as important, although it is not clear that the international experience resulted in increased independence; in fact, it may have been a characteristic enabling a person to join the Peace Corps. To use the Kauffmann, Martin, Weaver model, Peace Corps volunteers may already have been at level II of autonomy—inner-dependent (1992, 128). Ezekiel's (1969) study of volunteers in Ghana found that they were happier and more competent than their peers in the United States. Among other characteristics of the volunteers were self-confidence and responsibility. Smith (1966), who also studied volunteers in Ghana, similarly described their personalities as self-confident and responsible. The characteristic of self-confidence was also used to describe returned volunteers recruited into inner city teaching (Washington, 1964).

Another characteristic related to personal growth, which appears occasionally in the research, is what the AFS Study labels adaptability: "the ability to deal flexibly with and adjust to new people, places, and situations; willingness to change behavior patterns and opinions when influenced by others" (Hansel, 1983, 7). As with critical thinking and independence, flexibility was significant only among students in the AFS study who had no previous travel experience. Stitsworth (1988) also found an increase in flexibility among the 4-H travelers.

A quotation attributed to Mark Twain states that "travel is fatal to prejudice, bigotry, and narrow-mindedness," and Adler suggests that new attitudes will be the result of a transitional or international experience. However, the documentation of attitude change is difficult. (Note also that attitude change is related to the perceptual understanding category of gaining a global perspective—open-mindedness, as opposed to narrow-mindedness.) According to reviews of research, attitude change toward other countries and cultures has seldom been verified and seems to be affected by other things besides the international experience, including the facts that students go abroad with different attitudes and personalities, that length of stay varies, and that contact with host country nationals also varies (Hansel, 1984; Sell, 1983).

In a study of high school and college students who went to Europe, Smith concluded that "an unstructured, heterogeneous intercultural experience does not have a significant impact on general social attitudes." He wrote that "knowledge of a person's pre-existing attitudes appears to be a better predictor of his response to a heterogeneous intercultural experience than is information about the intercultural experience itself. The person who is most likely to become more world-minded and less ethnocentric following such an experience is the individual whose initial social attitudes are relatively conservative. The person who is exceptionally ethnocentric and nationalistic before he goes abroad tends to become even more ethnocentric and nationalistic" (1944, 477). It should also be noted that sometimes students' more negative attitudes about the host country after an international experience are the result of ideal image meeting reality.

Leonard found positive changes in attitudes after surveying five groups of Adelphi University students. She concluded that foreign study and travel "can produce a much greater change in attitude in a far shorter time than can a regular program of campus study" (1964, 180). The Adelphi students were abroad for seven or eight months, a longer sojourn than the travel of Smith's subjects. However, in a study of Youth for Understanding exchange students who were asked whether they had changed as a result of their two-month homestay experience in Japan, changed attitudes toward others accounted for more than 40% of the responses (Detweiler, 1984).

Besides length of stay, amount of contact with host country nationals varies. The Hoffman and Zak study mentioned earlier tried to relate change in attitudes toward another nationality with amount of inter-personal contact a person had with people of that nationality. High contact did make a difference. The high contact group had a significant average increase in their affect toward Israel and Jewishness, while the low contact group decreased or remained constant in their affect (1969).

Seeing the potential for changing attitudes through international experience, Kelman concluded that "the exchange experience is most likely to produce favorable attitudes if it provides new information about the host country in the context of a positive interaction with some of its people" (1962, 78).

DEVELOPING SELF AND RELATIONSHIPS: INTERPERSONAL CONNECTIONS

There is interesting and varied evidence about the existence and value of contact, beyond change in attitudes. James and Tenen noted, in a study of interaction of schoolchildren with persons from African countries, that if "interaction occurs, the interpretation concerns itself primarily with acts, words and expression involved in friendly or unfriendly behavior. But if interaction does not occur, then fixed characteristics such as colour and other physical features, habitual facial expression, dress and manners become more important" (1951, 60). Bjerstedt found that there were "clear tendencies toward less over-preference for the subject's own nationality and own language groups at the end" of an international summer camp. There were also more stories with cross-national references (1962, 25).

Studies on cross-cultural experience of young people also show interaction with others. Stewart (1976) found that New Zealand AFS students became substantially more social over the year. Kauffmann, Martin, and Weaver list a number of studies which have associated an increase in interpersonal skills with study abroad. They conclude from their interviews with students that "some opened themselves to a broader range of people, some changed friendship groups upon return, and others improved their communication skills, which enhanced their relationships with existing friends and helped them to make new ones" (1992, 106).

But what does this interaction lead to? Smith concluded that "persons who establish close personal ties with Europeans are significantly more likely than others to engage in internationally oriented activities following the European experience" (1954, 477). Smith's follow-up study (1957) found that behavioral expression of cross-cultural friendship, as measured by correspondence and sending of gifts, happened because of the development of intensive personal relationshps. *A Profile of the American Student Abroad* (Koester, 1985) showed long-term intercultural relationships as one result, with a longer stay (3 to 12 months) and direct participation in a foreign educational institution providing more opportunities.

In a study of the impact of the Fulbright experience, Burn (1982) found that three-fourths of the Fulbrighters to Germany had formed permanent friendships with people in that country. About 75% also sought out nationals in the United States from Germany and 65% assisted foreign students who came to their area. The Gullahorns (1960) found a correlation between the number and frequency of Fulbright lecturers' professional interactions with their hosts and their satisfaction with the Fulbright experience. After returning, about 80% of the grantees had entertained colleagues from their host institutions and others they met while abroad.

It is not only Americans who find interpersonal relationships important. In a cross-cultural confirmation of dimensions of intercultural effectiveness, Abe and Wiseman (1983) found that the ability to establish interpersonal relationships was one dimension of intercultural effectiveness for Japanese sojourners in the United States. The ability to establish interpersonal relationships had already been designated as one of three dimensions facilitating intercultural effectiveness for North American sojurners (Hammer, 1987). Another study listed interpersonal communication skills contributing to effectiveness as: flexibility toward ideas of others; respect toward others; listening and accurate perception of the needs of others; trust, friendliness, and cooperation with others, calm and self-control when confronted by obstacles; and sensitivity to cultural differences (Hawes and Kealey, 1979). Note again the overlap among categories in the model: interpersonal connections require the perceptual understanding of the global perspective.

Peace Corps research has also dealt with social interaction and interpersonal relationships, not as a result of international experience but as one part of effectiveness. Fuchs (1967) saw Peace Corps volunteers as engaged in caring relationships. Smith (1966) described volunteers in Ghana who liked their students and treated them with warmth and understanding and who showed consideration in their dealings with adult Ghanaians. Harris (1973), in an evaluation of effective volunteers, mentioned facility in interpersonal relations as one important characteristic.

Knowles (1970), looking at returned Peace Corps volunteers (RPCVs), saw a creative and practical orientation toward problem solving, especially in interpersonal relationships and involving cross-cultural differences. Washington (1964) was pleased with returned Peace Corps volunteers' positive attitudes toward aspirations of students and their sensitivity to other people and to group dynamics. Wilson (1986b) found RPCV social studies teachers agreeing that the following characteristics were common both to being an effective Peace Corps volunteer and an effective teacher: accepting of and relating to all kinds of people; adaptable/flexible; awareness of and respect for differences; able to deal with problems; caring; and openness to new ideas and experiences.

Of course, one does not have to go overseas to have interpersonal relationships with people of a different culture, and there is some research to show that cross-cultural social participation or interaction between American and international students is significantly related to acceptance of cultural pluralism (Sharma and Jung, 1986; Stohl, 1986), support of internationalism, a cosmopolitan world outlook, and world-mindedness (Sharma and Jung, 1986).

Sharma and Jung administered questions in seven areas, including those above, to students at four universities and compared differences between groups differentiated according to the amount of interaction with international students (no interaction; low interaction—one to three; moderate—four to ten; and high—more than ten). They found large differences even between students with no interaction experiences and those students with low interaction activities, and concluded that "interaction between student cultures does facilitate and encourage an international outlook" (1986, 385).

The A.M.I.G.O. Project at Purdue University is a deliberate attempt to give American college students some of the benefits of an international experience without going abroad. A second purpose is to provide a meaningful experience to international students in the English as a Second Language program. Stohl's research on this semester intercultural experience determined that the American students became more accepting of diversity of differences, as noted above, and also felt greater responsibility to and the increased importance of foreign visitors to the United States and developed a sense of importance of and a desire for travel abroad.

A third study, of a conversation partner program in which teacher education students were matched for a semester with students in an English as a Second Language program, showed that the future teachers gained in the areas of substantive knowledge and perceptual under-standing, *and* learned how to develop a cross-cultural interpersonal relationship (Wilson, 1993).

One interesting note. Although teachers who have been short-term international sojourners responded very positively to a survey statement that "understanding of other people comes through interaction between people," only slightly more than a fifth actually gave examples of interacting with people of different cultural backgrounds after their return from study tours (Wilson, 1984). The international experience of RPCV teachers seems to have had more impact in perceptual understanding (they accept differences), while that of short-term sojourning teachers seems to have had more impact in substantive knowledge (they use their new knowledge in the curriculum) (Wilson, 1986b). Purpose of the international experience and length of stay may be factors in the difference.

BECOMING A CULTURAL MEDIATOR

The discussion of interpersonal connections of Peace Corps volunteers and returned Peace Corps volunteer teachers leads to consideration of the possibility for internationally experienced persons to become cultural mediators.

In his examination of the effects of living in another culture upon individuals, Brislin lists "improved ability to act as a cultural mediator" (1981, 2). He gives as examples people who act as guides for sojourners to their own country and people who mediate between cultures by creating opportunities for monocultural individuals to communicate with their counterparts in other countries. Foreign student advisers and interpreters play the mediating role in a formalized way.

The concept of the mediating person as a bridge between cultures has been explored in a series of essays edited by Stephen Bochner (1981). The personality of the mediator is described as having characteristics now familiar, such as world-mindedness, self-confidence, and adaptability. "Above all else," writes one author, "the successful mediator must be tuned in to the satisfactions and dissatisfactions, the joy and the pain of those with whom he or she may be working" (1981, 244). That author also notes an important truth about intercultural mediating: "If I am too obsessed with caring for the other, I may become a nuisance, a missionary and be rejected or the other may become so convinced of the mediator's sincerity that he permits acts of exploitation" (1981, 228). Several authors write about the need for mediators to be culture builders, to be creative synthesizers rather than just translators.

One full description follows:

Becoming a mediator is often a question of being in the right place at the right time. Mediators carry their own cultural identity with them and function within this framework. They have their own vested interests, and are participants in the situation while maintaining sufficient detachment from it to understand what is going on. They too are adapting as they go along. Patience, goodwill, a sense of humor, and above all a basic respect and caring for persons—empathy—which one communicates are the tools of the trade. Mediators can perhaps sensitize those around them to cultural differences, or if they are planning, can plan in such a way that adaptation is fostered. Mediators can form bridges over cultural gaps. But each person must walk across the bridge for himself. (Bochner, 1981, 297)

Stonequist, in *The Marginal Man*, saw some persons as particularly talented at being what he called the intermediary in cultural relationships. These were marginal people, on the edge of two cultures. Some of his examples were minorities in the United States. He saw these mediators transforming the relations of races or nations from within outwards because of an ability to look at problems from more than one viewpoint. "His is an unconscious boring from within by which the underlying conditions are slowly changed so that new attitudes and accommodations become inevitable. His work belongs in the category of the slow, silent changes of history" (1937, 182).

The concept of "cross-cultural mediator" as a role for the Fulbright professor was explored by the Gullahorns who found that the position of the Fulbright grantee as equal-status stranger allows flexibility. For example, as a visitor, the Fulbright professor may be permitted the variant behavior of inviting students to his or her home which allows for informal, cooperative, noncontrived, and recurring interaction leading to positive cross-cultural attitudes (1960).

In the Peace Corps literature, Hapgood and Bennett (1968) use "agent of change" as a term to describe the role of volunteers. Their definition is offered in opposition to other concepts of the Peace Corps role, such as "the good seed" and "the international sit-in," and includes abilities which fit with cross-cultural mediation as well. Those are the abilities to adapt and apply improved productive technology, to understand the local culture, to explain the intruding world culture, to increase the options of the aided, to increase the power of the hosts and to limit one's own. However, Hapgood and Bennett conclude with a much weaker and perhaps more accurate metaphor for volunteers, "a subtle spice," more likely to be tasted in their own society. They point out that the United States needs people "who have successfully lived and worked in cultures radically different from their own to explain that wide differences in the way people do things do not necessarily spell defeat for the dream of human progress" (1968, 20).

Returned Peace Corps volunteers do act as cultural mediators. In a survey of RPCVs now teaching social studies, the respondents agreed with the following statements made by interviewed returned volunteers: Students who have traveled feel good talking to me as a teacher who has traveled (86%); I encourage students to apply for exchange programs (86%); My cross-cultural experience has made the transition of foreign students in my classes easier (76%); I attack problems of students from an environmental or cultural perspective (76%) (Wilson, 1986b).

Returned exchange and study abroad students have also become cultural mediators by befriending exchange students in their high schools or international students on their college campuses, by reaching out to people of other cultures in the community, and by participating in formal programs. Sometimes the cultural mediation or bridge-building is done with persons from the host culture. So a student helps a Japanese woman with shopping in exchange for Japanese lessons. Sometimes the bridge-building is generalized to other cultures. American exchange students returning from a homestay experience in Japan wrote about such experiences as teaching English to the music teacher's Panamanian wife, helping a man from Laos buy a fuse, and participating in the resettlement of a Polish couple (Wilson, 1985).

Not all internationally experienced persons become cultural mediators. The Study Abroad Evaluation Project uses the concepts of maximizers and minimalists. Maximizers incorporate their European study into their career values and employment practices. Minimalists value their foreign experiences but do not see them as relevant to their current work. About 60% of their sample were maximizers, about equally male and female, about 70% in professional/technical occupations such as secondary school educator, international attorney, composer and performer, and the rest in managerial/administrative occupations. Five groups of maximizers were identified: those in educational institutions; those in transnational structures, independent professionals, maximizers of small changes in complex organizations, and the deeply committed but situationally constrained (Carlson and others, 1990, 1991). Smith (1991), in her study of "the absentee American" who grew up overseas, describes repatriates as relativists, global citizens, and often wanderers. She sees potential for these internationally experienced persons to serve as mediators, and notes that many are employed in bridging occupations, such as teachers, consultants, trainers, and counselors where they can add their global perspective.

IMPLICATIONS FOR UTILIZATION OF INTERNATIONAL EXPERIENCE IN THE SCHOOLS

If schools and school people recognize the increasing diversity of the school population and the need to prepare all students to live in a global society, then one challenge should be to take advantage of the internationally experienced persons already in the schools—both teachers and students. Schools can draw on the talents of the internationally experienced in substantive knowledge and perceptual understanding and in personal growth and interpersonal connections.

Since schools are in the knowledge business and we live in a world of exploding information, the need for utilization of the knowledge of internationally experienced persons seems obvious. The Report of the Study Commission on Global Education (1987) recommended that four curricular areas be emphasized so students can function in our changing nation in our changing world.

1. A better understanding of the world as a series of interrelated systems: physical, biological, economic, political, and informational-evaluative.

2. More attention to the development of world civilizations as they relate to the history of the United States.

3. Greater attention to the diversity of cultural patterns both around the world and within the United States.

4. More training in policy analysis both of domestic and international issues. (1987, 3)

Internationally experienced persons are most knowledgeable about their host cultures (Area 3), but they may be able to contribute to other curriculum areas as well. Can they talk about environmental protection in Norway or business practices in Japan (Area 1)? Can they show slides of Gothic architecture or the Dachau concentration camp (Area 2)? Schools need to find out whether they can and then encourage teaching which includes sharing of that knowledge.

While perceptual understanding will be evident in the presentation of knowledge, it seems particularly relevant to curricular Area 4, policy analysis. The Report of the Study Commission on Global Education affirms a strong connection between citizenship education and education with a global perspective. The point is made that citizens of the United States need to participate in public policy decisions, and students need to be prepared to make public policy.

> Students should actively engage in analytical and creative thinking at all levels of the school program, sharpening their ability to recognize concepts, problems, and issues, to define them, to identify information needs, to analyze alternative solutions, to calculate costs and benefits, and to make responsible public choices. (1987, 20)

There is evidence that internationally experienced persons have grown in the various aspects of their perceptual understanding, such as critical thinking, reflective thought, perspective consciousness, and open-mindedness. Therefore, one contribution they can make in the classroom is to model that more complex thinking. Having dealt with different points of view, having developed a tolerance for ambiguity, having learned to observe and look beneath the surface, the teacher who did her student teaching in Colombia can tell about conversations with Colombians on the topic of U.S. foreign policy with regard to Central and South America. The teacher who was a Peace Corps volunteer in Sierra Leone can wonder about the efficacy of our foreign aid and the role of women in agricultural development. The returning exchange student from Japan can start a discussion about differences in schooling and ask what can we learn from them and what can they learn from us. Knowledge is still being shared, but it is being used to initiate discussions about issues by bringing up viewpoints beyond those usually found in the American classroom. Having someone talk about how Sweden deals with the issue of child care adds to the complexity of the thinking about an important issue. Still another way to make clear the complexity of world issues is to encourage immigrants and persons with international experience in the same country to discuss their views; they will, of course, not always agree.

Independence and self-confidence are areas of personal growth which seem enhanced for American young people by international experience. Internationally experienced students could lead and participate in activities such as an international fair, forum, or dinner and could speak to community groups and classes. Those internationally experienced persons with positive attitudes toward culturally different people could be a helpful leaven in a school setting.

The ability of internationally experienced teachers and students to make interpersonal connections across cultures is particularly important for schools, which already are and will increasingly be multicultural settings. Brislin suggests that "a long, close relationship with a person from another cultural group provides potentially powerful opportunities for learning" and that "one close intercultural relationship acts like a hurdle which, if crossed, opens up the possibility for other cross-cultural interactions" (1983, 536). The learning doesn't happen, however, unless the experience or the relationship is analyzed, reflected upon. While the one relationship "can lead to the development of cognitive complexity concerning the concepts of race, culture, and class and . . . to a more complex view of the problems inherent in prejudical feelings and intercultural interaction," Brislin points out that "unanalyzed experiences, sometimes due to such closeness to people from many cultures that 'the forest can't be seen for the trees,' are not necessarily opportunities for cognitive and affective learning" (1983, 536). Schools can have a role here in encouraging reflective thinking (discussion and writing) about international experience and about cross-cultural interpersonal relationships. Internationally experienced persons can extend their cross-cultural friendship experience on their own or in formal programs. They may serve as informal counselors for new immigrant and exchange students and advisers and officers for international and human relations clubs. So may immigrant and exchange students as they become more comfortable in the new U.S. culture.

The roles mentioned above show a capacity for cultural mediation. However, the term "mediator of culture" has sometimes been used in other ways. Traditionally, Grant points out, the "mediator of culture" has been "a person who both transmits knowledge of the culture and interprets the knowledge being transmitted" (1977, 85). Grant also argues that the role of "mediator of culture" has reflected ethnocentrism rather than cultural relativism; in other words, the transmission has been from a white, Protestant, Anglo-Saxon perspective. Some of Grant's recommendations for enhancing the mediator role are addressed in the model of the impact of international experience. For example, the perspective consciousness under perceptual understanding relates to Grant's first recommendation. Grant states that the teacher needs

1. to be assisted in learning how to face himself/herself;
2. to acquire the ability to analyze the nature and quality of his/her action in monocultural and multicultural settings;
3. to develop skills encouraging positive interaction among students of different racial and cultural backgrounds;
4. to advocate an education that is multicultural. (1977, 94)

Anthropologists have also written about the teacher as a mediator who explores how the task can be redefined for the framework of a student from a different culture. Writing about a Cherokee school, Dumont and Wax describe an intercultural classroom as a "locus where persons of different cultural traditions can engage in mutually beneficial transactions without affront to either party" (1976, 214). That definition fits better with the concept of cultural mediator described earler. The need for teachers who will be cultural mediators is certainly evident if we consider Kileff's (1975) hypothesis that where the social and cultural worlds of teacher and pupil overlap extramurally, the pupil will be more favorably treated in the classroom and Spindler's (1982) case study of a teacher who did not seem aware that he most frequently called on, touched, helped and looked directly at the children culturally like himself.

If teachers and students with international experience (as well as others who are able to be mediators because of multicultural family background or other life experiences) can be encouraged to bridge cultures in terms of substantive knowledge and perceptual understanding and can self-confidently lead in developing cross-cultural interpersonal connections, then students of minority and foreign cultures might be treated more sensitively and students of the so-called mainstream culture might learn from open-minded teachers and fellow students who do not think about either people or issues in simplistic terms. This would be no small contribution to the social education of young people who are going to school to prepare to be global citizens in the twenty-first century.

This chapter has shown that international experience makes a personal and, at least in the case of young people, developmental impact. International experience can also make an impact on schools when internationally experienced teachers and students have an opportunity to become cultural mediators. The following six chapters offer case studies of internationally experienced teachers and students at work in schools.

Chapter 3

Teachers with International Experience: "They Know More"

It makes it easier for her to teach 'cause she knows more about it and it's funner 'cause of the things she knows and we do. She talks about it so much I think she's from Italy.

He knows more than the book says. He can tell us what it's like to live there and bring things.

She would know if you put the Eiffel Tower in Italy. She knows landforms and history. She knows exactly how it is.

There's a big difference. You learn more from someone who's been there. We studied about Africa in Florida, but I learned more here.

These students are talking, at the end of the school year, about their sixth grade teachers and the difference that international experience made in their teaching of social studies.

What follows is the story of the teachers' school year, one year out of many interesting and productive ones. It is a story which illustrates how "role involvement or performance," in this case travel, contributes to knowledge shared in the classroom. It is a story which shows how teachers can use their international experience to teach with more accuracy, authority, creativity, enthusiasm, and understanding.

Angela Danner and Michael Worth teach at a three-year-old elementary school at the edge of a small border state city. The school is already bursting with 800 students who come from the low to middle income housing in the neighborhood, including public housing across the street. About 10% of the students are bussed in from upper middle class homes several miles away. Many students come from single-partent homes and homes in which both parents work and the families live from paycheck to paycheck. The students are mostly white, with each class having four or five African-American students and perhaps one Asian-American student. The principal and teachers have quickly built the reputation of the school, and it is a popular and respected assignment for students from teacher education programs at the local university.

THE TEACHERS THEMSELVES: KNOWLEDGE GAINED

Angela and Michael were chosen by the principal for the new school. Angela taught in grades one through four for four years in Virginia and Massachusetts before her two now grown children were born. In Kentucky she taught in a private kindergarten for three years as her own children got older and then returned to the public schools and taught in fifth and sixth grades at another elementary school in the same system for two years before teaching sixth grade at this new school. Michael started as a second grade teacher in an inner city school in the same system and moved with the principal of that school to the new school. During the year of observation, it was his first year teaching sixth grade and his sixth year of teaching.

Both teachers have master's degrees from local state universities. Both have undergraduate degrees from small, church-related colleges, Angela from a Virginia women's college and Michael from a Kentucky college. Both are active in the teaching profession and both have participated in federally funded projects in global education. Angela is active in the state and national social studies associations, and Michael has taught elementary methods classes at the college from which he graduated.

How they came to be teachers who could share knowledge gained through cross-cultural experience can be seen through their biographies. Michael grew up in a rural area and remembers that just riding the school bus to the nearby small town was a big experience. "As for what I learned at school about the world, there was very little." He remembers a textbook entitled *The Eastern Hemisphere*, but it made little sense because it had so little relationship to his own life. The teachers used only textbooks and never even talked about Europe and what was happening there. They were more concerned about what the rain would do to the tobacco crop and the news in their small town. Michael does remember that when President Kennedy died the principal came on the loudspeaker and said: "The President has been shot. This is of world importance. Let's all have a prayer for the president."

"But at college," reflects Michael, "I really began to be part of the world and live in the world. I took a cultural geography class where we had to learn capitals, rivers, mountains of every country. I also took a sociology class, and then I had an opportunity to go to Russia in my sophomore year. That's when the awakening came. I was so naive. When I went to New York City, I remember being downtown and I didn't know what a prostitute was and the women were trying to grab at you as you walked down the street. Riding the subway and taxis in New York and the trains in Europe—all for the first time. Going to the Soviet Union was exciting. I knew it would be totally different from the United States and I wanted to find out why it was different. I was exploring something most of the people at home didn't know anything about. On the way back from that tour I stayed with a German family for a week."

Since that first trip, Michael has been to Greece, Nigeria, England twice, through Europe on his own, and across the United States and Canada. "Every time I go," he says, "I think back. When I was in sixth grade, my world was right around me. Even when I started college, travel was so farfetched. No one I knew had been to Europe."

Angela's experience was different in elementary school. She had a fourth grade teacher who had taught in Alaska and "taught us all about Alaska." Her sixth grade teacher was married to an Army officer and lived in Japan after the Second World War. Remembers Angela: "Mrs. Hardy kindled interest in places other than Virginia. She told us that the Japanese used the edges of the newspaper for assignments and she was impressed by how much we wasted." Angela found a paper recently which she had written in high school about an imaginary trip to Europe. But at that time she thought she should see her own country first and traveling abroad didn't seem possible or practical to her in the mid-1950s.

The women's college she attended had only one program abroad which got started just as she graduated. For Angela the world began to open up after she married and moved to Boston. She and her husband lived in a cosmopolitan, racially and nationally mixed community around Harvard; they had Indian and Vietnamese neighbors. She taught fourth grade for two years and had a class in which one-third of the children had been to Europe. "I would mention Big Ben and the children had seen it and I hadn't." Angela's first overseas adventure was a two-month trip to Europe in 1970 and later she had opportunities to live in Rome on two of her historian husband's seven-month sabbaticals. The family also traveled extensively in Europe, especially in England and Scotland.

Angela remembers her first trip to Europe. "I didn't know the difference between Vienna and Venice. They weren't real to me. But going abroad and putting together what I had learned in books with what I saw was important. You can see an isolated picture of the Eiffel Tower, but when you're there in the rain it means something. Or, you can be at the Arc de Triomphe and see the ceremony honoring the unknown soldier and the veterans. You see that, relate to it, and understand what it must mean to those people. If you saw either picture in a tourist brochure, it would be only that, a pretty picture."

The knowledge Michael and Angela gained was not limited to those new cultures and peoples they visited. They also learned about themselves. Michael talks about the self-confidence he learned through travel. As with other young people, his first cross-cultural experience was a kind of rite of passage. Angela recognizes the self-confidence not only she but her children learned by living in Rome. "You have to get out and do what you can. You get a city map and a bus pass as soon as you arrive somewhere. Our children can do that now in major American cities, too. You also have to learn the customs of a place, like the siesta and restaurants opening at 8:00 P.M., and how to do without things. You learn patience and how to cope and can transfer that back here."

Michael and Angela also increased their interpersonal skills and connections, Michael by living with 15 people in a tour group in close quarters and Angela by living in an apartment of a Maltese Dominican convent in Rome. Michael says: "I was a loner in high school and lived in a room by myself in college because I didn't really trust people, but people accepting me as a part of a group changed my whole outlook." Angela remembers not only the Maltese nuns fondly but other experiences with people, such as Christmas breakfast with a teacher from Berlin in Amsterdam.

Cross-cultural experience, Angela and Michael discovered, is also self-perpetuating—one wants to travel more and learn more. "I came back from that first trip," remembers Michael, "with a drive to experience the new, to continue to experience different cultures." Angela talks about reading more about the places she's been. "When I was studying English literature I didn't understand why so many English writers wrote about Florence. I've promised myself I'm going to go back and reread and see what those people said about Florence."

Angela and Michael had gained knowledge about other cultures and experienced self-development and new interpersonal relationships. Could they be cultural mediators who transferred and translated what they learned in their classrooms?

THE TEACHERS IN THE CLASSROOM: KNOWLEDGE SHARED

The Material Culture

Already breathing her global perspective, Angela's empty sixth grade classroom awaits its occupants for the new school year. In fact, the janitor has tried to guess which countries are represented by the pictures in the hall wall quiz just outside the classroom door. Inside, on the orange, folding, all-bulletin-board wall there is a map of Kentucky showing towns like Paris and London and Athens and pictures of the European cities after which they were named. Also on that wall is a "Cruise the World" game and on a round table in the corner is a world map puzzle. A "Passport to the Sixth Grade" display, bordered by "hello" in different languages, is cluttered with name cards representing the places students will study during the year in social studies and pictures of those places. There are name cards for Greece and Egypt and Italy and pictures of the dye pits for cloth in Kano, Nigeria and of the Coliseum in Rome.

Across the hall in Michael's room a learning center entitled "Around the World in 180 Days" has been set up. On a tri-fold there are snap-shots from the teacher's travels with a challenge to try to identify the countries, and on the table there are travel magazines. A big globe perches prominently on a bookcase. There is a display of book covers representing stories about other countries. This room, too, announces that the incoming students will be learning about the world.

Activities in Michael's Class

The material culture is rich, but the teaching/learning interaction is another clue to the two teachers' abilities. During the second week of school the students in Michael's class are explaining news stories they have read. One student finds London on the world map, and Michael compares the cost of a Big Mac here and in London last summer. The assignment for next week is to read a news article that is not about the United States, and tell how that news affects lives in Kentucky.

In December, after the students have studied about ancient Greece, Michael is showing his slides of Greece. "That's Greece!" says a boy incredulously as a slide of cars and modern buildings is projected. "What do you see in this picture?" asks Michael. The students notice electric wires, television antennas, a parking lot, an Avis sign, a Pepsi sign, a soldier. The next slides show Greek Orthodox priests, then a flea market. A student asks, "Were things expensive?" Another wants to know if people ride bikes. Michael shows a picture of people whose home he stayed in when he visited Crete. "No, I didn't take pictures inside their house. That wouldn't have been polite." In answer to a student who asks, "Were they poor?" he asks, "What do you think? Are there dirt roads in Kentucky? Don't we have poverty, too?" He concludes: "We can't say our society is better than theirs. Societies influence each other, give and take."

Another day Michael introduces a decision-making activity. The instructions are:

1. You are going to travel to Greece. You will be spending six weeks on

one of the islands. Make a list of 15 things you would take. Remember your luggage can weigh only 40 pounds for an international flight. That's one suitcase and a flight bag.

2. Only 15 people can go from our class. Select the other people you would want to travel with for six weeks.

3. Choose what you would take to teach boys and girls of your age about life in America about each of the following: schools, family, food, fun.

During the discussion about things to take, Michael mentions the problems with electrical appliances like hair dryers which will have to be adapted to a different current. Michael asks the students to choose five things they can do without on their lists, and then five more. Still boys and girls both choose hair dryers. "Your suitcase might not close," warns Michael. When students say somebody might be hard to get along with, during the discussion of traveling companions, his advice is: "Take people as they are." During the discussion about what to take to describe the United States, he continually talks about travel as real and possible. "When I was traveling across Canada on a train and met two French Canadians . . . " "When I was in Nigeria . . . " "Someday you might get to travel . . . " He also refers back to what a Greek guest said in class. "What did Tina say about families and meals?"

Comparing past with present and here with there are constant themes in Michael's classroom. One day in February the students role play Roman patricians and plebeians and elect senators from their groups. Then they all role play senators and argue issues such as land, jobs, and equal rights as if it were Roman times. Finally, they talk about problems today. Students mention violence, jobs, housing, and Michael asks, "Did Rome have those problems? Will we crumble?"

The next month the topic is the Middle Ages. Michael asks, "What made society unfair back then? In what way is our society unfair today?" A student says, "Some people live in dipsy dumpsters." The teacher asks, "Is that the fault of society?" Other students say, "The poor are getting poorer and the rich get richer," and "Some people live in poor houses, but some people have swimming pools and tennis courts," and "There are not enough jobs," and "The President should get people working on buildings and not spend so much on defense." The teacher asks, "What is the number one problem in our city?" The students answer: "Pollution of the water," "Potholes," "Dirty streets downtown," "Need for jobs," "Crime—I had three 10-speeds stolen last year," and "My dad is a cop and he took me on patrol and we saw this guy with all these bottles." The teacher remembers aloud walking in Moscow at night by himself, something he says he wouldn't do in the city in which they live. He reminds the students about their Greek guest speaker who went downtown at night by herself here and later people told her she shouldn't do that.

In early April the students visit a nursing home. Michael explains that treatment of the elderly was one of the problems the students identified about their own society one day when he was talking about the role of old people in Nigerian society. Visiting the nursing home coordinates with studying the human body in science, too, and gives the students a chance to make Easter favors, tour the home, and each spend a few minutes talking with an elderly person.

Suddenly it is the end of May, and Michael has been accepted to go on a Fulbright study tour to Egypt which leaves the last day of school. "I'm going to pack my suitcase for Egypt right here at school," he tells his students. "What should I take?" Tony, one of the students, had confided the day before spring break: "Mr. Worth's been everywhere. He's going to Florida at 2:10. I wish I could go in his suitcase." Asked if he would like to go to Egypt, Tony replies, "Yea, I think I would."

Activities in Angela's Class

Angela's class is also an active one in which the scenery and the questions are always changing, although there are persistent themes, In October there is a "United Nations" bulletin board display and a "Feed a Hungry World" bulletin board display. One afternoon, after pairs of students play a game called "Immigrant," there is a discussion of refugees. The Haitians, interned at a nearby federal facility, are mentioned. The teacher talks about a Vietnamese family she knows. The students are involved in a special program at another school on the United Nations. They have also developed a display for the library by cutting out pictures which represent what they have decided are the qualities of a good life. On Halloween, while the other classes are having parties, Angela's sixth graders do a food distribution activity with three apples in which three students advocate three different distribution possibilities, and then the students have to decide what to do. They decide to cut each apple in 30 pieces.

After her Christmas trip with her family to Los Angeles, Angela puts up a bulletin board with postcards from Chinatown, a Universal Studio tour guide in four languages, and a picture of the first landing site of the Spanish in Caifornia. A "Where in the World Did It Happen?" bulletin board on current events is eye-catching, too.

The last week in January one of the students brings a neighbor to class who emigrated from Greece to the United States 10 years ago and has been back to visit recently. She writes good morning and good evening in Greek on the chalkboard and the children repeat the phrases after her. She shows the children some books on Delphi and the Acropolis and then they ask questions. A student wants to know about dress, and after the guest makes the point that people dress up there for dancing as people in the United States do for country dancing, Angela asks the class, "What were people dressing like here a hundred years ago?" "Yes," she points out, "Dress has changed here and in Greece over time." When the guest talks about the drachma, Angela extends the discussion by using her own experiences with pounds in England and explains how one changes money.

In February, Rome takes over from Greece and history becomes almost life size with huge posters of the Coliseum and Pompeii and a big map of Italy, all of which Angela has brought back from Italy. Her snapshots of modern Rome, tacked on the orange folding wall, have personal notes. "The Spanish Steps all decorated for spring. This is a good place for a sack lunch and a spot to meet people from all over the world." Another reads: "My favorite—Piazza Navona, once the scene of chariot races. You can eat a great chocolate here." Still another note says: "Daily open market—food of all kinds—take your own sack and go from stall to stall." An Italian potpourri display on the outside cement block wall bulletin board includes Italian newspaper headlines on Reagan, the news of the Pompeii earthquake, a school lunch menu, a bus ticket, a movie page from the newspaper, prayers in two languages from the Vatican, and an ice cream shop advertisement.

When Angela shows her slides of Italy, some she bought, some she took, she says, "You're in the forum now . . . " and "If you go to Pompeii . . . " One afternoon after she has talked about various ideas for mosaics (the students are going to do mosiacs of paper and ribbon, inspired by various pictures in art books and on slides), Angela begins to talk about the catacombs: "Let me tell you about the Priscilla Catacombs I visited last year," she begins. "A nun in brown greeted us. She spoke English, German, French, and Italian. You have to put on your jackets and you don't leave the guide. There are miles of catacombs and electricity is expensive in Italy. The passageways are very narrow and if I hadn't been on a diet . . . " Then she asks questions like, "How would they seal the body? What does the fish mean?"

There are other countries to study—a special Nigerian unit in which the four sixth grade classes participate together, utilizing lots of guests and Nigerian names for everyone and an African meal of jollof rice and banana fritters, and then several weeks on the Middle Ages, and a notebook on European countries. Connections continue to be made. When the students go to a state park for a special overnight trip, Angela reminds them as they hike up a natural pathway through a narrow place, surrounded by stone, that the damp, cool, musty feeling is how a castle feels. Posters from Lufthansa of Bern and the Rhine River may be on the walls now, but a high school student who has made a trip to Haiti comes to talk to the class about his impressions. From their study of Nigeria the students recognize plantain which he mentions eating. There are news articles about the local Haitians on the bulletin board, too. The leftovers from previous units are still visible in May. On one student desk is a book *Say It and See It in Italian,* and next to it on another desk are football helmet stickers and a Nigerian nametag that says Ade.

In October Angela said, "I was talking about riding trains the other day and a kid said, 'Have you been everywhere?'" Of course, she hasn't and is acutely aware of that. But now, in May, she has been chosen to go on a National Council for the Social Studies trip to Greece for three weeks in the summer, so she will be able to keep on learning, gaining knowledge and things to share with her students in future years.

These classroom activities and the enriching of the material culture of the environment for social studies are fairly obvious. The impact of cross-cultural experience on teacher goals and on relationships with children is more subtle, however, and the two are related.

Beginning Where the Students Are

Both Michael and Angela talk about starting at the beginning, "where the kids are." They know children between 8 and 13 are ready and open to learning about the world, and they try to capitalize on that. In a previous year with second graders, Michael had taught about families in the community and then moved on to telling his students about the German family he stayed with and about Italian families he knew. He also told his students about his own background—a broken home, an alcoholic father, being adopted by a teacher. He is especially proud of a letter from a seventh grade boy he had as a second grader who said he wanted to travel someday as Michael has.

Like Michael, Angela has also taught children from many backgrounds. In one of her kindergarten classes, a class of 20, she had children from five continents. "You don't ignore kids from different backgrounds," she says. "You have to use their knowledge. You have to let them experience." She remembers the inner city school where children wanted to run their fingers through her hair and her kindergarten class making different foods and flags.

For most of the students Angela and Michael are teaching now, it is a challenge to make them aware of the world beyond their own lives. "I start at zero," says Angela. "I throw out the term Mediterranean, for example, and then begin to identify places." Michael remembers saying at the beginning of the year, "Today we're going to read about Canada, the largest state in the United States," and no one said a word. Gradually, the students got involved. One day Michael told his students to watch the news because he would be on television. "The next day I had them tell what they had seen on the news and then I explained that all the news was about me because it involved my world." Angela also tried to get the students to relate to both other people in the world and the world as a whole. "I teach about interdependence, though I may not call it that." For a Global Product Search activity, she had each of her students bring a shoebox of items from home which came from other parts of the world. Once she pointed out the global connections of a Scottish bagpipe; the ivory is from Uganda and the wood from Tanzania. Art is one of her favorite modes for encouraging appreciation of other peoples. She used a visit to the Armand Hammer art exhibit at the local art museum as one focus and showed slides from the National Gallery.

What are their goals? Michael states: "I wanted to make the world seem more real through my experiences and I did that. I wanted to make them see Russia not as a bad place but as another way of life for other people." Angela says: "I'm trying to achieve an awareness that there are people beyond the local mall, people who care about the same things in the same way, people who share the same concerns about themselves and the world."

International Experience and Knowledge

The two teachers are asked: "How has international experience made a difference in your teaching?" Michael reflects: "I was able to tell them more than the book held, to go beyond and even question the book as I talked with them. I was confident of my own knowledge and able to bring out interesting details to keep discussions lively." Angela points out: "I can speak with knowledge, in a way I can't when I teach science. I can teach about Europe especially effectively because I can tell my experiences."

The 50 students, perhaps the most expert judges of the experience in the two sixth grade classrooms, agreed with their teachers' self-assessments, as evidenced by the quotations opening this chapter. But their teachers not only knew more, and therefore shared and taught more. They also passed on enthusiasm for and interest in travel and cross-cultural experience to their students. Their students, in one sense, became apprentices to the role of international traveler. They learned that such travel would be a valuable and possible experience.

In end-of-school interviews, every student answered positively the question, "Would you like to travel to another country sometime?" Several were tentative and chose Canada or Hawaii. Some students were optimistic, some romantic, several a little confused, but many were quite articulate and enthusiastic in their responses.

I'd like to see what it would be like to live in another country. See the Fiats in Italy, then go to Greece and see the Parthenon, the ruins of the Acropolis. Go up those big, tall stairs. See if there were those gods like Zeus.

I've always been interested in traveling because I travel with my family a lot, like to New York and Gettysburg and Washington, D.C. Now I'm more interested.

I'd travel all over the place. The world's going apart. It's important to communicate with people so we're more together.

It would be "tough" to go to another country. You can't just live isolated in the U.S. You've got to know about stuff because it's going to affect you. What if the Russians invaded Saudi Arabia? It would be "tough" to be a delegate to the UN to hear other problems. Or maybe a senator.

I'd go to Egypt or Norway. It would improve my learning. Instead of me making assumptions I'd see what they really do.

I'd just visit. You need to know languages and other ways of life. If they conquer you, you'd have to know the language.

I'd go to South America. I like looking at the new. I know someone from Iran. Some are good, some are bad—it's like that over there.

Greece sounds kinda fun, for about a week. I just like it here.

I'd go to Ireland cause it's green and stay a year or two and I don't think I'd ever want to come home from Holland because it's so pretty. It would be an experience you would remember and fun.

Yes, I'd go to the Rome remainings for a little while.

You hear about other countries on TV and want to know something about them.

Everyone thinks the U.S. is the only place to live. We need to learn how other people feel. They may even live in a better place than we do.

I'd go to Greece and Egypt for about four months. We ought to get to know more about people in the world, like Russia. People can travel.

Yes, I'd like to live in England. It fascinates me.

I'd go to London. It's a big country with all kinds of places to visit. We have to realize the world's a big place and people are different.

A guy in our church has been to Ireland. Most people don't have the right ideas and you can find out what people are really like if you travel.

Stuff from other countries fascinates me. I've never been and I want to know more about them.

You should travel so you won't think your country is best, but other countries are just as good. If we think we're better and Russia thinks it's better, then there will be fighting. It could be nuclear and phew!

I'd go to Africa to visit with people. Both my mother's boyfriends are from Nigeria. It would be a different experience to live in another country.

THE NEXT YEAR

It is late August and time for another school year to open. Angela is breathlessly just back from Greece, deciding to start with modern

Europe in social studies this fall. Her "Kentucky and the World" bulletin board is already up. Michael has moved to another room down the hall. He is dreaming of a world map on the ceiling of his classroom. Will he again organize a whole classroom Nigerian museum, as he did with his second graders two years ago? Or will the special emphasis be on Egypt this year after his six-week trip there? Knowledge about the world has been extended for these two sixth grade teachers. They have learned firsthand about Greece and Egypt through their summer experiences and are ready to share what they have learned with their students and to model again the international traveler.

Chapter 4

Returned Peace Corps Volunteers Who Teach: Fulfilling the Third Purpose

Some teachers have gained international experience through short-term traveling and living abroad, as Worth and Danner in the previous chapter did. Other teachers have had other international experiences, for example, being in the military overseas or being a Peace Corps volunteer.

Between 1961 and 1981 the Peace Corps contributed some 62,951 work years to 4,721,400 third world students and so fulfilled the first two goals of the Peace Corps to meet manpower needs and to promote a better understanding of the United States (Landrum, 1981). But as Peace Corps Director (and later governor of Ohio) Dick Celeste told returnees in early 1981: "There is a third goal and, in many ways, it may be the most important. . . . It is a sad fact that, despite modern technology, the United States remains culturally isolated from the rest of the world. In this sense, we ourselves are citizens of an undeveloped nation." He urged a consistent, determined effort to achieve the goal of educating Americans about the people and cultures of the so-called developing world (Rice, 1981, 85).

Some returned Peace Corps volunteers have been working on that third purpose for 15, 20, 25, almost 30 years, but that "educating" has not been very well documented, particularly as it relates to teaching American elementary and secondary school students. The 10-year anniversary issue of the *Volunteer* stated that one-third of the 46,000 returned volunteers were teaching (1971). A survey found that of 2,000 returned volunteers, the largest number (32%) were working in the education sector (Winslow, 1977). A book commemorating and explaining 20 years of the Peace Corps commented that perhaps the most exciting and profound impact of returned volunteers was in the field of education, though using only university examples (Rice, 1981).

Some wrote in the 1960s about the hoped-for contribution of returned Peace Corps volunteer teachers to education (Ashabranner, 1968; Calvert, 1966; Knowles, 1970; Warren, 1967), but only occasionally were problems analyzed (Kozoll, 1968; Wilson, 1966). More recent books and novels about the Peace Corps have concentrated on the overseas experience. One more recent study of returned Peace Corps volunteers who teach social studies concluded that they were cultural relativists, aware of and accepting of differences in people and culture; that they utilized their experience in what they taught, not only in country-related topics but by focusing on concepts such as ethnocentrism, racism, distribution of wealth; and that they saw themselves as living examples rather than agents of change (Wilson, 1986b).

Kennedy (1991) says it well in her introduction to an anthology of Peace Corps writing.

> Most Volunteers returned to the United States and continued their lives with mainstream American pursuits. They take care of their families, they work and play and organize, own cars and lots of other things. They eat well—every day.
>
> But there is a profound difference. The returned Volunteers know—in some deep place of their consciousness—that there is another center, another definition of life, another way. Much like immigrants, they live with the complexity and the richness of another vision, and know they will never again see with only one (1991, 11).

In this chapter returned Peace Corps volunteer teachers—teaching in schools in Washington, D.C., Cherokee, North Carolina, and in other cities, suburbs, small towns—talk about the difference the Peace Corps experience has made in their teaching.

BARBARA DILLEHAY

Barbara has taught in Washington, D.C. since 1969. She was one of the first group of volunteers in Sierra Leone in the early sixties and among the first 450 back in the United States. Before using her Kansas teaching credentials and Sierra Leone Methodist Girls High School experience to be accepted into the Cardozo Urban Teacher Corps in 1969, Barbara worked as executive director of the student YWCA at the University of Minnesota, then back in Sierra Leone on the Peace Corps staff. She also got a master's degree in African Studies at Howard University. She teaches at an academic high school for 400 selected students.

Her classroom has a bulletin board entitled "Think Globally—It's Your World" and a Chinese map of the world—in Chinese. On the blackboard are addresses of the World Bank bookstore, the Museum of African Art, and the Freer Gallery, helpful resources for the students' country notebooks.

Just now her tenth graders are discussing the results of a small group decision-making activity in which they had to choose appropriate projects on which to spend four million dollars for so-called developing countries. They are becoming familiar with concepts like growth and equity. A student says: "If the government distributes food, it's not increasing productivity and the villagers would become dependent on the government. Sort of a welfare system." Another student chimes in, "If you give people food, they won't know how to grow it for themselves." A third student wants to clean up the water first and then buy minibuses for taking health care to rural areas. One group is in favor of a brick factory, while from the other side of the room a student makes a passionate plea for education.

After class, Barbara wonders if the students should have learned more about the cultures of the countries before she used the World Bank curriculum which focuses on economic development. Thinking aloud about the impact of the Peace Corps on her teaching and the impact of her teaching upon her students, she says: "I am sensitive to the fact that there are different perspectives. In class I talk about the African side of exploration and colonization. It's more than knowing about the economics of Sierra Leone." The impact on students? She remembers a mother who said her kids were talking about world problems at the dinner table. The previous summer seven of her students went on exchange programs overseas, most on scholarship, recommended by Barbara.

BILL DORF

Bill is tall and straight and has a neatly trimmed beard. He can be imagined as a basketball player; he taught basketball and swimming as a volunteer in Indonesia in the early sixties. He can be imagined as a soldier; he was in Vietnam from 1966 to 1969. He can be imagined as a professor; he has his doctorate in American diplomatic history and teaches freshmen at the local university at night as well as honors classes of high school juniors.

Bill tells about growing up in a Brooklyn tenement as the son of first generation immigrants from Germany. That has also influenced his teaching—as much as Peace Corps, as much as Vietnam. "I'm comfortable with foreigners because I was the son of immigrants. I was used to being different," he says, "used to dealing with home values and school values which were different. My immigrant parents have had an impact on me and my teaching. I won't accept arguments for restricting immigration. I talk a lot about the contributions of immigrants. Students here want to shut off immigration. I believe they'll work hard and make a contribution."

Bill's father wanted him to be a barber. Bill had no intention of going on to college, but athletics opened the door and he went to a Kentucky regional university and majored in physical education and history. Joining the Peace Corps after graduation, he found himself coaching in Indonesia with a Communist bloc world-famous track star as his competition. When the Peace Corps pulled him out of East Java because of Communist pressure, he ended up as a teacher-trainer at a Thai university for the last six months of his service. After a six-month tour through India, Egypt, and Europe, he came home and enlisted in the armed services. As a Cold War warrior since high school and after his experiences in Indonesia where the local newspaper portrayed him as a CIA agent, Bill remembers that he was "pleased as punch the fighting was happening." He had some good experiences during his three years in Vietnam. He was in the field for six months and then ended up in public information, writing division history and taking care of reporters. He came home in 1969, still committed to the war. After finishing his doctorate in history in 1976, he found the college-level job market in history closed and took a high school teaching job. Currently, he heads a large social studies department in a central Kentucky school of 1,800 students.

Bill is articulate about the collective impact of his experiences upon his teaching. "It makes it possible to see things in a broader context," he says. "For example, when we talk about early American history we read a book about John Winthrop and talk about his idea of a city set on a hill. I take that and expand it. Do Americans still think of themselves as a city set on a hill? What implications does that have? I pull down an old map with the U.S. in the middle and Eurasia split. That leads into geography. The students have the problem of not knowing where Africa is, let alone Sierra Leone. When we talk about exploration, I ask why if Europe was on the east coast China wasn't on the west coast. We talk about the Chinese thinking they were the center of the earth, the middle kingdom. We talk about our ethnocentrism and some of the dangers of seeing the world that way. The injection of a world view is constant. When I talk about why European settlement took place in North America, I list the reasons and the source of the immigrants. Then I take New Guinea as a hypothetical case. I say I have 6,000 acres and I'll give it to anyone who will live on it for five years. There's malaria and there are alligators and it's hot and humid. Then I point out that I can't get you to go because you are fat and happy, so setting up a colony would not be successful. So why did the English want to go to swampy, malarial Chesapeake Bay. What was happening to England at that time?"

He goes on. "I stress that American culture is not the only culture. When some student has his feet up on the desk pointing toward me, I point out that pointing the sole of your foot toward someone is a deep insult in some cultures. I show how you call someone in Indonesia, the hand turned down. You only call animals the other way. I end up talking about Indonesia several times a week."

Do the students like that? He answers, "The kids think that all my experiences are neat, but experience can be limited. Experience was not such a good teacher for me in terms of Vietnam."

Bill repeats that the Peace Corps helped him see things in a broader context. He explains his view of history: "I talk a lot about the past, present and future. I tell students they are surfers on a wave rolling through American history. Their parents put them on the wave. They have to understand that wave in order to stay on and not get dumped. I talk about the utility of history and the need for a historical perspective." He also pushes a global perspective. "I'm always on the kids for just eating hamburgers and coke. The world is bigger than the Dukes of Hazzard. We talk a lot about current events. I'm always saying open up, take a taste—eat artichokes and crepes—and travel."

Bill takes his own advice. He has traveled to France, his wife's home, during a number of recent summers, and his daughters want to go back to Indonesia with him.

MONA CAIRN

Across town from Bill in a low-slung junior high is a young woman in her second year of teaching science and her third year back from Peace Corps teaching in Samoa. "I grew up ten years worth in the Peace Corps," she says. She thinks about its impact and the impact of subsequent travel to Japan, Korea, Somalia, and Kenya on her teachng. "I take it a little easier and am more relaxed. When you see people ill and unable to get medical care, the importance of memorizing science vocabulary pales. I'd rather they stay interested in the world in science class than stomp on them."

She remembers being timid her first year in talking about her Peace Corps experience because she thought the kids would be bored. Her feeling is that people don't want to hear about such experiences, though some teachers once asked about the Peace Corps in the teachers' lounge. Still, Samoa does give her examples for teaching science. "I have great stories about the tides, about volcanic activity and earthquakes, and seeing the Southern Cross." Several months into the school year, she's talked about Samoa three or four times in classes.

Mona also brings her experience with individual differences on Samoa into the Kentucky classroom. "I think each child is special. I get upset with teachers who expect the same thing from the students. In Samoa I saw problems with different levels of English. That's a problem here, too, and I have to take that into account."

The future? Mona doesn't plan to retire in the school system because travel is in her blood and she has a boyfriend who is a medical student interested in going overseas. Still she likes Kentucky; she grew up in Connecticut but moved to central Kentucky with her family when she was in high school. "Living overseas makes you appreciate what is in the United States," she points out. "It helps you appreciate cultures here and not put them down as being country or hick."

ELIZABETH MAHONEY

Spanish class at the magnet School for Creative and Performing Arts in Central Kentucky begins as classes begin in Latin America. The students stand up and greet the teacher, Elizabeth Mahoney, who was a Peace Corps volunteer in Ecuador from 1981 to 1983.

The Ecuador experience is the reason Elizabeth earned a master's degree and certification in Spanish. She teaches the sixth, seventh, and eighth graders almost entirely in Spanish, from the *Gracias a Dios hoy día es viernes* (Thank God it's Friday) on the blackboard to her classroom management comments. The seventh graders do a rap song to learn capitals and countries of Latin America and leave the class singing a song of colors. The eighth graders work in pairs to do interviews with each other about their families and then have a follow-up assignment to write about an imaginary family in a particular Latin American country.

Elizabeth really wants to share cultural knowledge and global sensitivity. The students cry "Ola" and hug each other as they practice conversations. Extra credit is given for current events reporting from Spanish-speaking countries. A former campus Peace Corps recruiter and president of Kentucky Returned Volunteers, Elizabeth has linked her students, through the Peace Corps' Worldwise Schools Program, with a Peace Corps volunteer in the Dominican Republic with whom letters and packages have been exchanged.

Elizabeth compares herself to other teachers. Although 26 students crowd six tables in a small room, she says, "I'm just glad to have a classroom. Other teachers complain, but we have lots of resources." (She taught kindergarten classes of 42 students in Ecuador.) Elizabeth sees her Peace Corps experience as contributing to her interest in getting students involved with local and national, as well as international, development projects—recycling, a food drive, trying to make connections with a school in hurricane-devastated Miami. The Peace Corps also sharpened her interpersonal skills. "You learn there that interactions with people are as important as getting the job done. Here, with faculty, that means finding out where they are coming from. With students, it means relating Spanish to other things in their lives." Finally, Elizabeth is committed to changing attitudes, especially toward other people. She wants students to understand that other people are more like us than different from us. She wants them to look beyond life in the United States and what's good for us and to be aware of the effect we have on other people.

Elizabeth and her husband, a returned Peace Corps volunteer whom she met in Ecuador, have a two-year-old son and another baby on the way. In the summer of 1992 they took 10 middle school students to Mexico for eight days. "I enjoyed it enough, I would do it again," says Elizabeth.

KARL LENTL

After nine years teaching in Tunisia (the first three with the Peace Corps), plus three years in inner city Cleveland, and four years running outdoor education programs for a camp, Karl is now teaching fourth grade in an exclusive suburb in northern Ohio.

This day his students are dressed up to participate in a United Nations Day to which parents have been invited. The girl representing Mexico lived in Monterrey for two years; the girl representing Lithuania has the costume because her father was born there; the girl representing France was born there and goes to Düsseldorf, Germany every summer to visit relatives; the girl representing Tunisia is Karl's daughter. One boy shares what he brought back from Saudi Arabia several months ago, and another student talks about going to Switzerland in the summer. But Karl is happiest about a boy who hasn't traveled but has dressed in a flannel shirt to represent Canada; it is important that he is participating. Karl says, "The collage of children's faces through the years is what keeps you going."

Like Bill, Karl points out that one's whole life history infuences one's teaching. "I already had an enthusiasm for different lifestyles because I had grown up in Oberlin as the son of a college professor and I had been a camp counselor at a camp for inner city children, but Tunisia enabled me to maintain that enthusiasm. I think if more teachers had a variety of experiences, such as Peace Corps, they would have more enthusiasm and be able to make things more meaningful. There isn't a day goes by that I don't use my experiences. Today we were talking about communication in a story we were reading and I talked about the fact that three months ago I called my friend Beshear in Tunis and he sounded like he was next door. I have lots of memories of real people. So someone talks about oranges and I tell my story of riding on top of an orange truck in Morocco. I'm always saying 'Let me tell you a story.'"

Karl also talks about the past—taking students at the American school in Tunis where he was headmaster and teacher on outdoor Tunisian Studies field trips—and the future—plans for teaming his class with an inner city Cleveland class for some activities and setting up class exchange trips with France, and plans for living and teaching overseas again. His family, including his wife who grew up in Iran and his son and daughter, keep up their French; the children participated in home-stays in Quebec, and both became high school exchange students in France.

RAY AND CONNIE MCCLOUD

Across the city in another less exclusive suburb, two returned volunteers teach physical education and social studies at a high school of 3,000 students. Connie grew up in Cleveland and went to summer school in Norway as part of her college experience; Ray grew up in southern Ohio and graduated from Ohio State. They met and married as Peace Corps volunteers in Turkey in 1966. They lived in Oregon one year for Ray's master's and another year in England where Ray was on a Fulbright teacher exchange.

As they talk about themselves, the Peace Corps, and teaching, life history is again important. Connie says: "I don't know many teachers who were raised on welfare in a housing project. I've come from a threadbare background and I'm proud of what I've done. Because I was raised there, I met a lot of different kinds of people. I knew people growing up with so much more generosity and simpatico than the so-called educated people. They are really the deprived ones."

How has the Peace Corps influenced her? Connie answers: "Your experience gives you a distinct perspective. The U.S. is notoriously isolated. If that's your only experience, then your glasses are tinted by that experience. I don't just see an issue as an American but also as a Turk, a Briton, a Norwegian. And I'm not talking about a tourist perspective when you come back feeling superior about how cheaply you bought that copper tray." In school Connie makes a special effort to introduce new students from foreign countries (several recently from Greece) and ask that they be included. At the middle school she tried to teach Turkish folk dancing, but the boys were less than enthusiastic. She has also been translator and interpreter for a Turkish family who moved to the United States so their children could be treated for kidney problems.

Ray shakes his head. "To think what I would have been like as a social studies teacher if I had started teaching with just my small town Ohio experience. I don't think you can teach about the world without having experienced it. I draw the exchange students into my classes. I bring social workers in from the Council of International Programs exchange. I'm talking about universal public education in American history and I end up talking about Turkey. When I taught a unit on Turkey as a middle school teacher, I brought in a Turkish TV guide and said to the students, 'Now you tell me about lifestyle changes in Turkey.'"

Neither Ray nor Connie found their fellow middle school teachers very interested in recognizing their experiences. Ray had been asked to speak about Turkey to another class only once in 15 years. The high school teachers seem more "worldly" and interested in teaching about the world. In fact, in the spring of 1992 they were both involved in a special Global Education Day at their high school, sponsored by the returned Peace Corps vounteers in northern Ohio. In the future, the McClouds look forward to a Fulbright exchange for both of them.

JENNY AND MILT WHALEN

Jenny and Milt taught in the same school system as the McClouds for seven years, but since 1975 they have lived on their own small farm in rural northern Ohio. Jenny has been an elementary counselor; Milt teaches math half-time and counsels half-time in a school of 180 students, K–8. They both originally grew up in a small town in western Ohio and had married and taught before they went to Ethiopia to teach for the Peace Corps in the 1960s.

Milt is teaching seventh graders. Although he makes it clear they chose the rural lifestyle, not the teaching jobs, he clearly enjoys his students. Because Cheryl has checked her subtraction, he says, "You get a star!" Of another student who has missed a lot of problems he says, "Renee did a fantastic thing for us. Now you can all be scientists and figure out what she did wrong." Then it is time to go over long division. Milt sets the scene: "I come from another planet so you'll have to explain everything to me." The students come up with one explanation and then another and then a third student says, "Another way would be. . . ."

Later, talking about himself, Milt says, "People here know I march to a different tune. One of the teachers thinks when he refers a kid to me, the kid ought to get fixed. He's working on a medical model. I do a lot of counseling with teachers, saying you need to keep this kid with learning disabilities in your class and you may need to read his test to him and saying this other kid will have to be successful without doing her homework because I've been to her two-room house and there's no kitchen table to do her homework on."

What about the Peace Corps? Milt is blunt: "Peace Corps was the best two years of education we had." Milt talks about the Ethiopian experience as leading to teaching in a Cleveland suburb because that's where the power was and where the attitudes needed to be changed. "Living in significantly different cultures makes you appreciate differences," he says.

Jenny's first cross-cultural experience was as a 17-year-old AFS exchange student to Norway. "I think Milt would say I pushed Peace Corps." She talks about the impact of her experiences on her work as a counselor. "The big thrust of my work was to get kids to accept differences. I could do that because of the experience of being a minority person in Ethiopia." She wants students to learn tolerance for other ways of doing things, for people who are different because of culture, handicap, different social standing.

The conversation continues. Peace Corps volunteers were agents of change in other cultures perhaps. The questions are: "How is one an agent of change in this culture? How does one influence values without alienating people?" "Nobody is offering me a contract to promote change in this community," Jenny says. And yet she and Milt are doing it, very gently.

JERRI FULK

Not everyone who joined the Peace Corps was a recent college graduate or was married or came home to have two children, as the Whalens and McClouds did. Jerri, who has just celebrated her fiftieth birthday happily and proudly, was almost 30 when she went to Cameroon as a community development volunteer on a two-year leave of absence from her high school teaching job in a small Ohio town. Except for those two years and two earlier years teaching in Germany at an army school, she has always taught in the same high school—first social studies and later English.

She is a big woman physically and laughs about being called "Big Mama" in the Cameroon and being regarded as a sex symbol for the first time in her life. Peace Corps experience brought Jerri prestige back home as well, and she still talks to community groups and gives guest lectures on polygamy and child rearing in home economic classes.

After visiting her class, which is reading *Things Fall Apart*, by the well-known Nigerian novelist Chinua Achebe, there is time for continued conversation at her home as she makes West African palm oil stew for supper.

"Before I went to Africa I was an intellect," she says. "I became intuitive. I have always had a good instinct for teaching, but I learned to trust my intuition more. I always had close relationships with kids, but that's even more true now. I don't join everything anymore—that infernal business. So I have time to be around when kids need me, even in the middle of the night. Last fall someone was trying to commit suicide, and kids sometimes want to talk about problems in college."

As if on cue, the phone rings and she talks at length to a would-be poet, a former student now at a nearby university. Then she continues: "I am more sensitive to non-verbal communication and observe body language and behavior. I see past what students write. The Cameroon experience made me distrustful of words. I found out until I sincerely respected people, I couldn't communicate."

Jerri describes the "mishmash of people in this town" and says, "you can't treat them all alike. Because I went to live in a different culture and saw different cultures even within Cameroon itself, I learned to look for differences." So, although some of her experiences and insights are different from those of other volunteers, learning to look for and accept differences is a similarity.

CARIN FRAY AND SARAH WALTON

In a university town in Illinois, two women are utilizing their Peace Corps experience as they teach students for whom English is a second language. Carin was in Sierra Leone from 1976 to 1978 with her husband, who is now working on a doctorate in science education. They spent a year biking around Europe before joining the Peace Corps and are considering living overseas again. Sarah met her husband in Thailand in 1974 where she was teaching English; he was traveling through after a VISTA stint in American Samoa and now sells insurance. Carin started out as an opera major and switched to elementary education. Sarah majored in Asian Studies and English at a small liberal arts college and went on a mind-stretching world-tour seminar before getting certified to teach. After a year teaching 12-year-old third graders in a Chicago ghetto, she joined the Peace Corps on a dare by her father.

Carin, who is working on a master's in English as a Second Language, splits her time between the high school program and working in an elementary school. As she sits at a round table in the bilingual classroom of the elementary school, a child comes in who's been tripped on the playground. She hugs him and gives him and several others a task to do at another table.

Carin compares herself to her partner at a previous school situation, where she had become a tutor after a neighbor in university housing said she would be good because she was culturally sensitive. "I would ask, 'Why did so-and-so do this?' and she'd say, 'Oh, he's a discipline problem.' For example, we had a problem with a Greek boy who was refusing help from a younger tutor. But I had lived in Greece for three months and thought his ego was involved and he was offended because his tutor was younger. I told him I had never seen behavior like his in his country since in Greece one respected wisdom as well as age and that I thought he was behaving inappropriately for a Greek. It worked. My partner never considered culture. But I learn about cultures I haven't known anything about before." Carin points to the bulletin board with a Thai poster, information on the Vietnamese holiday Tet, and flags from Germany, Thailand, Vietnam, Venezuela, Cambodia, and Sierra Leone—the nations represented in the bilingual class. Three of her students have just presented a Columbus Day assembly, telling about their trips from Vietnam, Laos, and Germany to the United States.

Carin reflects: "I haven't always been like this. I was born with the prejudices and stereotypes of the south (in southern Missouri). Anything black was bad. I never had the courage to go across the tracks until after college when I was teaching in a Title I black school. Then I tried to make up for my earlier prejudice by tutoring in student homes. I was a caring person before I went to Sierra Leone but I went through cognitive changes so that now I see relationships between language and culture. I am aware of errors and interferences. I do not think errors are bad. Some may be made as part of a process of understanding. I never considered that until I lived in a Sierra Leone village and made lots of errors myself. Now I think of the intent of the error." Carin stops to answer a child's question and then continues: "I also know meaning is not just in the structure of the language but in the way I stand. All languages have patterns but the meaning is culture specific. Everything is related. I think the main effect of the Peace Corps is that I am not a one-dimensional person."

Sarah has been running the bilingual program at the high school since 1975. She has 37 students in a pull-out program three hours every morning in the cafeteria and also teaches several classes of psychology. Three certified teachers and three tutors work with her in teaching a curriculum that includes—besides English—health, U.S. History and Civics, and consumer education. She begins the morning with 16 students studying Copings 6 in the consumer book. She goes over advertising claims and terms with the students, using herself as an example and laughing at herself, and then asks the students for examples. There are other smaller classes working at other cafeteria tables, and she talks loudly and dramatically to keep students' attention.

Like Carin, Sarah attacks problems from a cultural perspective and she is slow to make judgments. She tells about a teacher diagnosing a student as dyslexic because he was writing from right to left—he is an Arab and Arabic is written from right to left! She points out the aide who that morning wanted to know what's wrong with Ton That—Sarah is reluctant to say anything is wrong because she knows the family and knows they have just had more members of their family arrive as refugees. She tries to help other teachers appreciate the refugees' culture and their situations. "If they just realized the family lost two brothers over the side of the boat on their way to the United States," she says.

Her international experiences make her students' transitions "about as easy as they could be." She speaks Thai to the Laotians and they speak Laotian to her and they understand each other. "I loved the Thai, they loved me," she says, "and it's the same here." Finally, there is her sense of humor. A favorite story is how she told a Thai cab driver she was a "banana" instead of "afraid."

BOB HENDERSON

Bob is applying for jobs as a high school principal. He'd like to help teachers set their own goals for self-improvement and development. He believes leadership is critical and is concerned about what he sees as the condoning of racism.

At the moment Bob is teaching history, specifically the Peloponnesian Wars. "Education courses affected my teaching more than Peace Corps," he says. His students are answering questions about causes and results of the wars by using two texts which make contradictory statements. However, Bob admits that his Peace Corps experience—teaching in and being principal of a junior secondary school on an island in Fiji in the South Pacific—gave him a different perspective toward things. (He joined the Peace Corps because a bad eye and a bad ear meant he was rejected for pilot training.) "Now cultural relativism," he says, "is part of my personality. I just accept that kids are brought up differently." His high school in a Michigan town across the border from Toledo, Ohio has a large minority of Hispanic students, and he has six exchange students in his classes.

Bob says he talks more in classes about Latin America and Europe and his travels there than his experiences in Fiji where he taught from 1968 to 1970. That seems a long time ago—and yet Bob is considering doing a dissertation on the history of multicultural education (he has master's degrees in both history and education and course work done for his doctorate), and he talks about the importance of equality among people with religious intensity. He also remembers with pride students in the early 1970s who took all his electives—in Mexican history and minorities and World War II and anthropology. "There are five kids I influenced one helluva lot."

SALLY SELNICK

Teaching English in rural Kentucky seems unrelated to being an educational supervisor working with educational television in Colombia. Sally is married to the head basketball coach of a county high school and lives on a farm with her family.

Sally occasionally speaks to school and community groups about her Peace Corps experience. She talked about styles of clothing at the FHA banquet. She has spoken Spanish with students in the school who are from El Salvador and Guatemala and notes the Spanish words in a short story the students are reading in English class. She would like her sons to be exchange students, but her husband is not especially excited about international experience.

A very hardworking teacher, she is sponsor of the newspaper and worked with cheerleaders for 13 years. She is especially proud of a yearbook dedication to her a number of years ago which reads in part: "For the past two years, Mrs. Sally Selnick has encouraged, sacrificed for and loved each of the members of the staff. For this enthusiasm and guidance dedication, we love you." Sally says, "You have to really care."

A link to her experience in Colombia is her 1990-94 four-year term as the teacher representative on the statewide Council on Educational Technology. She got that job after participating in a national telecommunications project which linked her class with one in Maryland. Their project to exchange was a video which showed what the students learned from research on the changing economy of their county. The project was later showcased in a magazine ad for PBS. One summer she did 25 days of training in technology. She is also a resource teacher for new teacher interns. Says Sally, "I'm a lifelong learner and willing to take risks, try new things—like being in the Peace Corps."

LETITIA DOWLING

Peace Corps experience seems even more remote to Letitia, who has been a classroom teacher and is now a librarian at an elementary school in a small Kentucky town. She has fond memories of working in community development in Honduras. "I told a marriage counselor last summer," she says, "that I felt more comfortable with Peace Corps volunteers than any other people I've been around since."

Sitting in her classroom-size library, with books lining shelves on every wall and under every window, Letitia talks about growing up poor and ostracized because of an alcoholic father, working her way through college, learning Spanish in Peace Corps training (she hasn't used it since she left Honduras), and trying to stay married to a diabetic husband with values different from her own. "I hope I'm different," she says. "I want to be different. I don't want money to be my road to happiness. In this society it's you do something for me, I'll do something for you. I want something done freely, with no conniving. It's so easy to get in that rut. I have to stop and think."

She recalls doing units on Latin America and Mexico when she taught fifth grade, but can't see that the Peace Corps experience has influenced her as a librarian. Then suddenly she thinks of a book and finds it on the shelf. It is entitled *Lito, the Shoeshine Boy*. "The photographer has captured the way it is in Latin America," she says. She took it home to read to her son. Letitia is thoughtful. "You don't erase that whole experience."

ALLEN MAYFIELD

To the west, in the city of Louisville, right downtown, few of Allen Mayfield's students know he has lived in Africa or have ever heard of the Peace Corps. But Allen's experience with a crafts program in Upper Volta (now Burkina Faso) made him want to teach, and an interview while visiting friends for the Kentucky Derby got him his post-Peace Corps job teaching art.

Allen grew up in Texas; his parents were poor, and his grandparents lived on a farm. He had his first experience in an integrated situation as the only black student in the art department in college. Then he lived with a white volunteer in Upper Volta and was seen as a white American in Africa. "So I can relate to black and white kids equally well," he says, "and I have all kinds of friends. I am a model in some ways to some of the black kids because I believe anybody can do anything. I got my self-confidence and self-image from the Peace Corps." Like Sally Selnick, Allen talks about caring about kids. "These kids have problems you wouldn't believe, but some teachers have never been to the West End. Teachers also make fun of kids who are gay. Other teachers put themselves above kids. I have a feeling for kids and their problems." He continues, "I contrast the appreciation there in Africa and the not caring here. After seeing the poverty in Upper Volta, I know making it is possible. People make excuses for poor kids, but poverty has nothing to do with minds."

Allen considers the future: it is time for a change. He is tired of teaching. Maybe they will move to Houston, maybe even overseas. Allen and his wife were planning to go to Senegal on vacation several years ago but had a baby instead. "I have no idea what or where," he says, "but to be rich is not important."

MARIE WAY

Marie, elementary physical education teacher in Cherokee, North Carolina, sees herself as different before she went to Tunisia as a Peace Corps volunteer and as different still. She is half-Cherokee and grew up in Cherokee, respecting both her Indian grandmother with traditional beliefs and her non-Indian relatives whom she visited in Canada. She credits the experiences of growing up respecting the beliefs of others and seeing poverty on Indian reservations as preparing her for Tunisia in a way her fellow volunteers, mostly from eastern colleges, could not have been prepared. Before she joined the Peace Corps, Marie had gone to boarding school in New Mexico (where the dorm matron was a returned volunteer from Peru) and to teachers colleges in Kansas and North Carolina. She also did student teaching in Asheville, North Carolina.

Marie is also different from her Peace Corps compatriots because she came home. "The majority stayed in Arab countries," she says, "or joined the foreign service. I'm the only one so far who is married." She has three young children and stays in her present job because she wants the good things of life for them. She plans to switch kids for a summer with an English friend. For herself she dreams of attending the language institute in Asheville and going into health administration.

Marie is also different from her fellow teachers because she is from Cherokee and still lives there. Parents often come to her instead of other teachers. She is very involved in the community, saying she stays so busy because Cherokee is "so dull. The only way to cope here is to do things as fast as I can." She coaches gymnastics and does volunteer counseling on a teenage hot line, dealing with drugs and pregnancy; she also teaches a "straight Sex Ed course" at the high school. She loves doing craft work and going to craft fairs and makes feather combs with Indian relatives.

The impact of the Peace Corps? "I don't ever talk about it," she says. "People in this environment wouldn't understand. I've refused to speak to groups. They're not interested in Tunisia; they have no concept of Africa except barebreasted women and jungle." And yet Marie sees the connections between her Tunisian experience and the Native American experience. She talks about her assignment in a boarding school in the mountains where she taught 200 girls who were being trained as nursery aides. "It was like the Indian reservations when they went and got the students, said they had to go to school, and didn't pay attention to what happened to family life."

She doesn't talk about Tunisia with students, but the "thing I stress with my own family and with the kids I teach is—just because you don't believe it or understand it doesn't mean it's wrong. I want to help people be more tolerant of each other. I don't think you broadcast that. I think you have to live it."

SAM POUNDER

Just down the road at a K–8 school that is off the reservation and 50% Cherokee is another former Peace Corps volunteer elementary school teacher. Sam is also from the mountains, from the Virginia Blue Ridge where his parents owned a country store. He got a liberal arts education at William and Mary (math major) and two weeks after graduation took his first airplane trip to Lesotho, South Africa.

In Lesotho he became very interested in teaching. "I had 90 kids for triple periods in math class to get them ready for the exam and 75% passed." Sam decided he needed a teaching degree and went to the Teacher Corps office as soon as he returned from Lesotho. They said he needed more experience so he became a social worker for several years, working with child abuse. He was hired at the school near Cherokee after a two-year Teacher Corps internship there.

"Peace Corps was the best thing that ever happened to me," Sam states categorically. "It acted as the catalyst to the multicultural already in me." He bounces with enthusiasm as he talks about the effect of Peace Corps experience on his teaching.

"I know experience is important to kids," he says. "I've also become a better listener and that's characteristic of my teaching, too. I do some show and tell but I also listen and let students find their own way. I'm more aware of international events and can't get enough information about what I want to know. In class I'll say, 'Hey, did you all hear about . . .?' I teach the kids Lesotho counting to get their interest. I still hold up three fingers the Lesotho way if I'm counting three apples, for instance. In science, I tell them about the highly developed color sense of the Lesotho. There's not just black and white or brown and white and red but color names for each combination.

He describes his contribution to other teachers' classes during an African unit. "I come in speaking only Sesotho (the language of Lesotho) the first half hour and then show slides—not only exotic ones. I ask students to figure out what 20 slides they would take to show their home and school and the United States and then they realize how hard it is to see a country with a few slides. I get at the stereotypes of lions and jungle." Sam has also spoken at programs at other schools and to women's groups and church groups.

A teacher of the gifted and talented in the morning, he teaches math and science in the afternoon. Although he concentrates on math and science in the gifted and talented program, he also teaches language— Sesotho, French, and German—and creative writing. He asks students to invent a culture, too, and then compare it to Indian and African cultures. He finds the Indian students are especially interested in asking questions about African cultures.

Sam has kept and increased his contacts overseas. "When another teacher takes in my mail during the summer," he says, "she is fascinated by the postmarks from Germany, England, Kenya, Lesotho, Sri Lanka. Last spring an English couple visited me for two weeks and went to school several times. The students and teachers were interested in them and asked later how their American travels had gone."

In the summer Sam continues his travels. He helped with an ecological study of the Baha desert in Mexico one summer and made another month-long visit to Mexico in a van. During the year he is tutored in French and German twice a week. He also takes every opportunity to speak out on international affairs, especially apartheid in South Africa.

Looking for further growth, he's considering going to Saudi Arabia to teach. Sam remembers his high school French teacher who always said, "When you get to Paris. . . ." He also tells his kids not "if" but "when." He got to Paris, and he expects some of his students will get there and other places in the world, too.

Chapter 5

An Afghan Sixth Grader: "Making My Country Remembered"

Not only teachers bring international experience to school. In many schools across the country there are immigrant and refugee children who struggle to make sense out of American culture, but who also bring their international experience as a possible contribution.

Schools usually make the assumption that they should "help" immigrant and refugee students, and they do in a number of ways. They provide English as a Second Language programs all day, partial day, pull-out tutoring. They may try to make students feel more at home by offering bilingual programs. Occasionally, they organize a supplementary lunch hour course on cultures in transition or show films about students' native countries. Less frequently, schools recognize that immigrant and refugee students can contribute to the school's program. For example, a teacher at a high school in New York City, which has an immigrant population from 100 countries and where almost half the 3,200 member student body comes from homes where English is not spoken, incorporated the Great Decisions program from the Foreign Policy Association in his social studies classes. He found that emphasizing the contemporary world in a regular American studies class converted the immigrant students from outside spectators to inside participants (Wilson, 1986a).

This chapter is the story of one immigrant student and his sixth grade year. It is not told because it is a typical story, but because it is a particularly hopeful one which represents the synergy of an internationally experienced student and an internationally experienced teacher in one classroom.

In late May Jimmy talked about himself and his second year in the United States. "This year has been a lot better," he said, "because I can speak better English. I got friends here and people are helping me with my English . . . Especially my teacher has been helpful. She talks about Afghanistan and tells every kid about it. She does special things like last Friday (Afghanistan Day) and in the middle of the year, too." A darkly handsome, lithe boy wearing jeans, T-shirt, tennis shoes, and a Michael Jackson jacket, Jimmy talked confidently about going on to junior high and about college, too. "I think it will be fun to go to junior high because it makes you feel like you're big. You learn different things and you can have your own locker. You can play football or soccer. I want to go to college. Maybe study computers or be a doctor."

Jimmy's arrival in central Kentucky almost two years earlier came after several years of mobility—escape from the Soviet invasion of Afghanistan during which his affluent family saw their possessions confiscated, a two-month stay in Pakistan, one-night stops in Turkey and England, and two years in Gross-Gerau, Germany. There he attended German schools, learning to speak and read and write that language, while waiting for his father, already in the states, to obtain visas for the family. By the time Jimmy's grandfather on his mother's side arrived, in the middle of Jimmy's sixth grade year, the family group in central Kentucky had grown to about 25. Jimmy's immediate family included an older sister, a younger brother and a younger sister also in elementary school, and a baby brother.

Jimmy's grandfather had been a businessman with houses in Kabul, the capital, and Kandahar, another major city. The Kandahar house had 33 rooms, 4 baths, and servants, and the grandfather had traveled to the United States, England, and Germany, as well as to countries in Asia on business. Jimmy's father had imported trucks and owned a store for bathroom fixtures in Kandahar, but came to the United States before the invasion. Along with several brothers, he worked at an Italian bakery and restaurant during Jimmy's sixth grade year.

When Ahmed (as Jimmy was known in Afghanistan) enrolled in fifth grade, the principal suggested he be called Jimmy, and so, in the tradition of many other immigrants and refugees, Ahmed got a new name. The following summer the family moved to a housing project in another part of town, and that fall Jimmy found himself in sixth grade in another school.

THE TEACHER

The sixth grade teacher's first concern for Jimmy was to deal with his need to communicate, although he seemed quite fluent verbally. She arranged for a math tutor and a reading tutor. Probably more important, however, she also decided to keep Jimmy in her class all day for all subjects except science which she did not teach, although he was thus in the "wrong" math group. Another sixth grade teacher emphasized word and logic problems in teaching math, and she realized language would be a problem then even in math, which is generally a fairly universal subject. Besides, in a self-contained situation, follow-up was easier. Between classes Jimmy was able to sneak in a quick tutoring session, especially in math. Sometimes he asked for additional explanation or an assignment. Other times he simply sought reassurance that he was following directions correctly. Finally, the teacher kept Jimmy because she recognized her own interest, experience, and flexibility in dealing with children from different cultural backgrounds in comparison to her fellow teachers. From her point of view, the class was fortunate to have Jimmy as a member. She had taught Vietnamese refugees and children of IBM executives from Mexico in sixth grade before. She had also lived overseas and believed she was aware of and accepting of cultural differences and was willing to be flexible in how she taught Jimmy. "Antonyms are so hard," she noted in an October conversation. "I just put an X in my gradebook for him for that skill and we'll go on."

Jimmy's teacher's first actions were management decisions, based on her perception of his needs and her interest in him. How she dealt very naturally with Jimmy as a member of the class but yet as an individual with special needs is also instructive.

First, she explained assignments, activities, and words carefully. In a language arts lesson in December, for example, she checked with Jimmy several times about meanings of words, including "require," "cooperate," "complex," "distributed." During that hour-long lesson he was involved 10 times by being called on or getting a special explanation or as a topic himself, as when she used the spelling word "occur" to introduce a future happy event when his grandfather was due to arrive from Pakistan.

A second way in which the teacher helped Jimmy learn was by making relevant comparisons for him and by encouraging him to do the same. While showing slides of Greece, she suggested that Delphi could be compared to Mecca. When she discussed Greek pottery, Jimmy raised his hand and explained, "In Afghanistan they make pottery and drink water from it, but it's brown and doesn't have pictures." Earlier, during the unit on Egypt, after the teacher had described ways of getting water from a well, Jimmy described drawing water from a well in Afghanistan. After an art demonstration on weaving, Jimmy brought his book on Afghanistan and said, "See, we weave, too, and make rugs."

Jimmy participated in the regular curriculum, of course. Near Halloween he drew pumpkins and a witch, following the other children. During a discussion about the election, he said he had seen the new governor on television. Near Christmas, he participated in a play reading about Santa Claus. He was attentive when the students watched the filmstrip version of "The Door in the Wall" during the unit on the Middle Ages in Europe.

The teacher also put Jimmy's experiences into the curriculum. On October 26 she said: "I was going to wait to involve Jimmy until later, but I think I'll involve him now." The impetus for her decision was Jimmy's comparison of his way of writing to the Rosetta Stone.

Two days later a section of the bulletin board was entitled "What Can We Learn about Afghanistan?" The headings were: Government, Music, Language, Writing, Religion, Food, and News. Jimmy had written his Afghan name, Ahmed, in Pashto. Stapled on the bulletin board were a picture of a mosque from a tourist brochure, pictures of various cities, and a newspaper story about the Soviets in Afghanistan. Another article with pictures described archaeological work in a northern Afghanistan tomb, comparing it to the Tutankhamen tomb in Egypt. There was also a world map with Afghanistan circled. On a table in front of the bulletin board Jimmy put two books, one on carpets and another general one published by the earlier monarchical government.

The teacher introduced the bulletin board as an ongoing project and then asked Jimmy to write on the blackboard his name and the name of the country in Pashto and to pronounce them. She also talked about different spellings and pronunciations of Rome, implicitly saying that "different is okay." Students noticed Jimmy wrote from right to left. A lengthy discussion ensued about different languages and people students had known from different countries. One student remembered a Swedish girl from the previous year who "learned English real good." Another remembered Apu from Bangladesh, someone else mentioned fellow sixth grader Chi, born in Vietnam, and still another student remembered David form Germany. "My dad is tutoring some people from Argentina," said one boy. Jimmy got involved again to tell about Afghans who go to Saudi Arabia because their religion is Islam. During the discussion, the teacher pulled down the map and pointed out the countries they were talking about. A positive feeling about people from other countries was pervasive.

The bulletin board display remained up all year, and Jimmy added items, such as money, to it occasionally. He seemed to feel it was "his" spot. Afghanistan was frequently mentioned, especially in comparison to other countries studied. Jimmy would speak up in class discussion and say, "We have that kind of flower in Afghanistan" or "We pray in our house five times a day" or "The teachers in Afghanistan are very strict." In January as the Greek party and Olympics were being planned, Jimmy said his mother would cook some food for it, but the teacher told him they would have a special Afghanistan Day later.

That morning in May designated Afghanistan Day, students did various tasks concerning Afghanistan geography, the flag, and Arabic numbers. The teacher began the lesson by relating the Soviet boycott of the Olympics to the American boycott protesting the Soviet invasion of Afghanistan. Jimmy told what he remembered of the invasion—the tanks and the people wearing red to show they were on the Russian side, but his family wasn't. Jimmy then served food his mother had prepared, including huge pans of subtly spiced rice topped with carrots, raisins, meatballs, and tomato, cucumber, onion, and lettuce salad. He served it to the other teachers, too, and the principal.

While Afghanistan Day was the highlight of Jimmy's contribution to his classmates' introduction to his country, his History Day project which traced his family's journey from Kandahar to Lexington was his contribution to the community's education about Afghanistan. As in her decision to keep Jimmy in her class most of the day, her care in explanations, her encouragement of comparisons, and her inclusion of Afghanistan in the curriculum, the teacher was motivated both by her own curiosity and her concern for Jimmy as an individual when she suggested he do a History Day project. "It was a story that needed to be recorded," she said. "I saw the project as a natural for a student with a story to share. The History Day theme of 'Family and Community in History' also made it a natural."

Working with another boy who was a good student as well as neat, organized, and interested, Jimmy developed an exhibit which included magazine pictures, personal photos, maps, and written accounts of his life in Afghanistan, Pakistan, West Germany, and the United States. His special tutor assisted him in correcting the written account as part of his composition lessons. The project won third prize in the History Day regional contest, and Jimmy and his partner proudly wore their bronze medals to school the next week. The project and the boys were the subjects of a school television segment and were featured on the local newspaper's Kids Page the following month. The exhibit was displayed at the International Fair at the university, at the local library, and at the school district central office.

The teacher was obviously a major character in the story of Jimmy's sixth grade year. One might say she was the director and producer of the play. There is also a leading man or woman in most plays, however, and he, of course, was Jimmy.

THE PUPIL

One of the reasons Jimmy had a good year as a sixth grader was that he had a good teacher who, as Jimmy himself noted, had been especially helpful. Another reason for Jimmy's good year was his own motivation.

At the end of the year his teacher wrote: "From the first I realized he would not be a passive student. He had much to contribute. I have never before had a student who was so eager to learn, so motivated to succeed, and yet so eager to share the positive aspects of his own culture." In March she reported that Jimmy was so hard-working that he came to school early to be tutored so he wouldn't have to miss regular classes. The only time he missed school was an afternoon for oral surgery. He almost always completed assignments. When he heard his teacher mention that her daughter had a scholarship, he wanted to know what that meant. When he found out what it meant, he asked, "How do you get scholarships? When I finish high school, I will get a scholarship."

What were some examples of his eagerness to learn and to excel? He persistently typed in the same sentence on the computer, trying to get it correct, instead of playing the video game of zapping the rabbits like the boys before him. He learned the days of the week in Italian after the teacher showed him the *Italian Made Simple* book and was the only student to say "thank you" in Chinese to a visiting Chinese couple after they had taught the class. He did three projects on Greece instead of one, as well as a Greek vase which was displayed in the principal's office. He was upset on field day when he didn't get any firsts.

Jimmy's eagerness to share his own culture reflected his self-esteem. He knew who he was and where he came from, as well as where he was going. He did not seem marooned between languages and between cultures. He also wanted to "make my country remembered." Jimmy's face lit up when he talked about his family and about Afghanistan. In December he described the sheep they would get for Christmas, perhaps one for each family or perhaps several families would share. They would cut the sheep's throat themselves, he explained, and say some words and make some gestures, "like people do at Mass." Then they would slice the sheep and cook it in water and add spices. At Christmas the families would gather to drink coffee, milk, and tea. The children would get several dollars to spend. In Afghanistan the small shops would have been open on Christmas so children could buy things, he said. They wouldn't have a tree.

When he shared his books on Afghanistan, he pointed out the mosque in Kandahar; he showed a picture of Mohamed Zaher Shah, "the good king"; he remembered the camels getting in the way of the buses in Afghan cities as he pointed to a picture of camels. He was not at all happy with the book sent from the Afghanistan Embassy entitled *The True Face of Afghan Counter-Revolution*. "The Russians are not good," he said. "This book says the mujahadeen did things which the Russians did." When he made a poster for the PTA "I have a Dream" contest, it read as follows:

People need their freedom.

Each country needs peace.

Afghanistan needs its freedom.

Catch all the Soviet people and let us have our freedom.

Everybody wants freedom and peace.

He also mentioned peace and freedom in journal essays on Greece and on education.

While Jimmy was intensely motivated and intensely proud, he was also a normal boy who sometimes whined, "Do I have to . . . ?" He also fell in love with girls and wasn't sure he could miss a soccer game to go to the History Day contest. He talked to girls on both sides of him during math, horsed around with other boys at lunch, and played kickball enthusiatically at recess. He seemed to get along well with other students. As he said in the interview and wrote earlier in a journal essay: "I got friends here." That was one of the characteristics of the "lot better year," according to Jimmy. He wrote about one friend who was nice and "if you tell him something he won't say anything."

Research in bilingual education suggests some reasons why Jimmy became fairly fluent in English, another reason for the "lot better" year from his viewpoint. Children about 10 years old are fastest at language acquisition; Jimmy was 11. Personality factors such as the tendency to be outgoing affect language acquisition; Jimmy was talkative and friendly. Integrative goals (getting along with people in a new culture) and instrumental goals (getting a job, thinking about the future) are related to language acquisition; both applied to Jimmy. Parental support is important, and Jimmy's parents were supportive (Milman, 1984). Since lack of fluency in English seems to be an important barrier to positive social relations, Jimmy's fluency and number of friends are presumably related.

So Jimmy's driving motivation, high self-esteem, desire to get along with others, and improving English fluency made him, to a large extent, master of his own fate. Another metaphor is possible. He was an enthusiastic runner at the starting line. His teacher was the coach.

OTHERS

The sixth grade included 28 other pupils. The teaching situation was not a play with one actor or a coach with one athlete. The teacher admitted at the end of the school year: "Maybe he was a pet. But he was so interesting and so many kids don't do their work as he did. I had to watch favoring him. Sometimes I had to be a little mean. I talked to him when he got cocky. He was responsive to discipline." She pointed out that Jimmy's fellow students quickly respected him because he had had interesting experiences. They were impressed when he told what it was like when the Soviets invaded. They were also impressed with his language facility. A girl who went with Jimmy to his home to get the food his mother had prepared for Afghanistan Day listened wide-eyed as he switched effortlessly between Pashto and English.

Perhaps because the teacher modeled an interest in and respect for people from other cultures and for being bilingual, the students seemed to be interested in Jimmy and respected him. Out of 26 "Perceptions of Social Studies" questionnaires administered at the end of year, eight mentioned Jimmy and/or learning about Afghanistan in answer to general questions which did not ask about Jimmy or Afghanistan specifically. Responses included: "I have changed in my views of people in other countries, such as Afghanistan people because of Jimmy"; "From sixth grade "I'll remember the 'Afghan Taste' ' "; "I feel I know Afghanistan people now"; and "I know Jimmy and myself better."

Certainly the teacher felt that Jimmy's presence had served as a catalyst for learning experiences the whole year. However, the relationship was reciprocal. He opened the door to a new culture, while fellow students helped him learn a new American way of life. Some helped him with vocabulary and several tutored him in math. One student helped him organize and prepare the History Day exhibit and in the process learned a lot, too.

Also in the category of supporting cast or team members were Jimmy's family. They invited the teacher and her family for dinner during the first month. They made sure their children went to school every day. They had high goals for Jimmy, and his goals were high, too, both in terms of education/career and material success. He retained middle or upper socioeconomic class expectations; he said his father would buy him a car when he turned 16. The family was seen by the school as being education-minded and they were selected by the administration to receive a complimentary set of encyclopedias from World Book. Jimmy apologized for living in the "apartments," and, although he played with children who lived there, he was upset by alien values such as young, unmarried girls having babies. He felt the people around him did not have pride in the upkeep of the apartments. His family's religious values were important and he was not afraid to explain them.

Jimmy wanted his mother to sign up for classes in English. His mother had not gone to school, but she could read and "knew about religion," he said. She had talked about moving to Saudi Arabia where Islam would be the predominant religion. Jimmy's concern for his mother was apparent, and he clearly planned to do things for her when he grew up. He also saw himself as the leader among his siblings. He said his older sister didn't talk much and a younger brother and sister were too little.

His third grade brother may have felt pressured because he was behind a year, a decision made when the children entered American schools, and Jimmy's self-confidence may have fostered his brother's insecurity.

Jimmy's sixth grade year must be seen, then, as part of an interactive situation in which he had an impact on his classmates and they on him and in which his family was also important. The full cast or team has now been described.

From Jimmy's viewpoint, his "lot better" sixth grade year happened because he learned the language, he gained friends, and people helped him. His teacher, the chief helper, facilitated the learning of English formally by arranging for him to be tutored, but also by explaining carefully and encouraging him to make comparisons. His own motivation and self-esteem were critical factors from the teacher's point of view. Age, personality, and family support contributed.

However, it is not only the interaction of teacher and pupil which is crucial in this story. It is also important that the teacher and pupil—she with international experiences and cross-cultural awareness and he with pride in his home country and an eagerness to learn and to share—were able to bring the world into the classroom. Wrote the teacher: "Jimmy brought meaning to and tolerance for one of the world's great religions to a few children in Lexington." Said Jimmy: "They [his classmates] learned a lot of things about Afghanistan —food, clothes, language, religion. They ought to know about Afghanistan because it makes you feel better to know about other countries. Like I am from Afghanistan and now in these two years I know a lot of things about the United States." A fellow student wrote: "I feel closer to the people of Afghanistan."

Jimmy and his teacher offer a model for other classrooms, if a student wants to "make my country remembered" and a teacher wants to facilitate that student's learning and learning by other students.

Chapter 6

A Little United Nations School: It's a Natural

International experiences impact individual teachers, students, and classrooms, as is evident in chapters 3, 4, and 5. They can also impact a whole school.

"It's like working in a little United Nations," the first grade teacher says of Beech Valley School. "Every time I pull down the map they love it." A parent volunteer in the library, the mother of a second grader and a fourth grader, echoes the teacher: "It's wonderful! We have a little United Nations school here." Asked to describe the school, a fifth grade boy says, "We have a lot of foreign kids who are interesting. Like for lunch the Japanese bring rice cakes."

"In this school," reflects one of the gifted program teachers, "it's ordinary to have traveled. Sometimes I don't even know whether a child is a citizen of another country or not." The PTA president says: "So many kids have had cross-cultural experiences that it seems commonplace. My eighth grade daughter has an opportunity to go to Europe for the first time this Christmas to visit relatives. She's very excited, but her friends are quite blasé about it." A fourth grader says: "Lots of kids in my class have been to Germany, me and Lori T. and others. I have a friend who goes to Jamaica to see her grandparents, but nobody really makes a big deal out of it—it's just something they've done."

Beech Valley School, a K-6 public school in the affluent Washington, D.C. suburbs, serves 450 children who represent at least 40 different countries. About 25% of the children are foreign-born, but others have foreign-born parents, and many of the American children have traveled or lived outside the United States. The staff has also had diverse experiences. One teacher was born and educated in France and another was born and lived in New Zealand until she was five. One teacher lived in Japan and Panama as an "army kid" and in Germany as an adult; he is fluent in Spanish. The librarian spent two summers in Mexico; he is determined to become fluent in Spanish. Most of the teachers have traveled in Europe, several have been to Israel, and previous teaching locations include North Carolina, Ohio, New York City, and Alaska.

The principal, who grew up in a family where Italian was spoken, was sent to Italy at age 19 to study for two years. He has also had a Fulbright to Venezuela, spent a summer in Mexico, and traveled in Europe and the Caribbean with his family. He looks upon the school's international dimension as quite natural. Schools where he worked on Long Island and in Miami also had an international flavor, although he admits this school is "skewed more that way." In his office he flips through the enrollment cards and lists various countries. There are about 20 children from Japan and about 20 from Brazil. Four children from Greece are currently enrolled and one from Finland. (A tally based on returns from an International Parents Club questionnaire and other information shows that there are approximately 12 Latin American, 8 European, 10 Asian, and 4 African countries represented, plus Australia and New Zealand.) Later, pointing out students from other countries on the playground, the principal seems almost surprised at what a worldwide group he oversees. There is a student from France, another from Sri Lanka, a third from India. Two girls are playing a hopscotch-like game and chattering in Spanish. Two boys walk by, talking earnestly in Japanese.

So what happens when a principal, some teachers, and many students in a school have had cross-cultural experiences outside the United States? How does this little United Nations school work? Why does it seem natural or ordinary?

INFORMAL AND FORMAL CURRICULUM

Coming in the low, red brick school, the visitor is first struck by "Welcome" painted on the wall in various languages: Gia Sou, Jambo, Dag, Adab, Wilkommen, Shalom, Ciao, Ahu Yong, Merhaba, Konnichiwa, Hola, Oi, Hello, Bonjour, Aloha. The halls are bright with large bulletin boards showing off student projects, interspersed with prints of famous paintings by artists from Gauguin to Tanner which the principal urged the PTA to purchase last year.

Just past the teachers' lounge and the math resource room in the English as a Second Language room, the poster on the bulletin board announces "Friends Around the World, Sharing, Caring, Growing More Beautiful." The teacher herself announces: "There's a meeting at another school next week and they need welcome signs for the meeting." Her two Greek students and one French and one Japanese student begin to make the signs. The Japanese student explains that there are three kinds of Japanese writing. He goes to Japanese school on Saturday and so has no time to play soccer. "C'est magnifique!" the teacher says of his artistic characters. To one of the Greek boys she says: "Your brother was trying to teach me Greek this morning. Do you remember we talked about the phrase 'It's Greek to me' last week? Maybe you can say, 'It's Japanese to me.'" Later she concludes: "There goes our lesson for today, but this has been very interesting. I learn so much from you kids."

In the library some fourth graders have a reference lesson, looking up answers to the librarian's questions in the almanac. They are trying to discover, among other things, facts about various world religions, how many of the Declaration of Independence signers were born outside the United States, and to what country Americans travel most often. The answer to the last question is Canada, but a child from China would like it to be China. There is some confusion about whether Protestants are also Christians.

At the check-out desk at the other end of the library, a fifth grade student from Peru is checking in books. Her English is not fluent enough to do the "Weekly Reader" in the classroom so she and another Latin American student have some free time in the library. They speak Spanish to the librarian and he answers them in Spanish. Then someone comes from the fifth grade to tell the students to return to the classroom. The Peruvian girl waves at the other Latin American student. "A la clase."

In a small room off the library/media center, autobiographies written by children in the primary gifted program are displayed on the bulletin board. "I went to Room [Rome] with my Dad," says one. "We also visited friends in Germany. We went to Nebraska at Christmas to see my grandfather." Another reads, "My father is a diplomat. I was scared to come here at first but the plane was fun."

Across the hall in the first grade classroom, November and Noviembre are on the bulletin board. The lesson on the blackboard is titled "Nutrition," and foods from Germany, China, Mexico, and Peru are listed. The reading group sitting with the teacher is looking at pictures of Venice in the reading book. "Did your parents go to Venice when they visited Italy?" the teacher asks one of the students. On the other side of the classroom an American student is doing a comparative writing assignment on "my store" and Josephina's store," based on a reading book story. He understands the differences in what one could buy at the two stores from reading the story, but he doesn't know where Haiti is and yams sounds strange to eat.

Back down the hall and across from the office, in a sixth grade social studies class, the students are working on individual plans for an ancient city. Their teacher spent three summers at Tell Gezer in Israel as a member of an archaeological dig. The students have seen the slide tapes he made from his experience. There is a bulletin board, too, with pictures he drew and snapshots from the Tell, as well as a student imaginary dig diary from a previous year. Later the students will play a game he developed called Archaeological Grid in which each small group discovers and draws various items on their section of the grid and the groups put together the sections and share what they have found. Leaving at the end of class, a student says to the teacher: "I'll meet you at Gezer."

"This kind of opportunity made history more exciting for me." The teacher evaluates his dig and travel experiences 12 years earlier. "You have to know your content and be excited to get kids excited." He begins to get excited as he talks. "There's just something about being there. I got to Delphi and found a stadium and theater at the top. It wasn't as small as I had thought. And to be at Masada—oh gee!"

So cross-cultural experience is evident in the teacher-student exchanges and in the planned and unplanned curriculum. When teachers and students and parents begin to identify ways they remember cross-cultural experience has been utilized in the classroom, the list grows far beyond the planned curriculum. One teacher remembers the son of the ambassador from Burundi explaining how he helped his father with the cattle at home and collected cow dung for fuel; the teacher then made a comparison to the American West and the settlers' use of buffalo chips. Another teacher tells about one fourth grader teaching beginning abacus and some of the Japanese characters to his classmates and a second fourth grader, from Sri Lanka, reporting on how tea is grown and how elephants are utilized in agriculture as well as on how the complicated governmental system of his country works. The same teacher has asked American children who go abroad, even on a skiing trip, to keep a "compare and contrast" journal to share when they return.

In the sixth grade during the study of the development of civilizations, students have dated events according to Hebrew, Arabic, and Chinese calendars. One boy wrote his grandparents in California to get a Chinese calendar for the class. Personal magazines which one sixth grade class constructs at the beginning of the year include sharing of cross-cultural experiences.

Sometimes a speech assignment or a project is a vehicle for telling about one's country. For a speech assignment, a sixth grade Nigerian student told about her grandmother, who was the first girl from her village to go to school. In the primary gifted program, an Indian student designed a museum on spices.

The sharing of cross-cultural experiences may be incidental to class discussion and then may depend on teacher encouragement. A fifth grader says: "Sometimes teachers ask, sometimes I raise my hand. When they talk about archaeology, I can share from my experience in Kenya." A sixth grader from Greece says: "Today they asked about the Greek gods—did we still worship them? I gave my social studies teacher some pictures of Greece. He's been there. In language the teacher asked me to say some words in Greek and then to say a story in Greek and the students had to try to figure out what I said." An Egyptian student says he has never been asked to speak or write Arabic, however, and an American boy, back from a year in London, says no one has asked about his experience there.

Teachers have experiences to share, too. The librarian does some of the teaching for the third grade unit on Mexico, talking especially about the family he lived with during his summers in Mexico and their daily routine. "The information in the social studies book is correct," he says, "but the impression is wrong. The children are learning about the native costumes and taking it literally. They need to know that some Mexican kids wear jeans to school, too. They need to be studying not just the problems of the lower class but the middle class. We do have one set of filmstrips which show middle class everyday life. Our students also need to study young people, not just games and folktales. The kids are interested in school life in other countries. If we just teach them folktales, they think people sit around telling folktales all the time. Having fiction written by someone who has lived in the country is helpful."

The fourth grade teacher who has lived in Japan, Panama, and Germany often relates personal experiences. He emphasizes current events because he wants all the kids to become aware of the world and to develop a worldview. "Awareness is important," he says, "even if it doesn't lead to appreciation. At least the students will not have uninformed or misinformed opinions."

The principal, who was once a high school world history teacher, enjoys sharing his expertise, too. He teaches about Rome for several days as part of the sixth grade curriculum.

The context of all this sharing of experience is important, of course. A fourth grade teacher talks about her emphasis on comparison as the class studies state history. She also stresses similarities: "Everybody has laws and a religion. The differences are so small in comparison to the big ideas." A fifth grade teacher relates a different philosophy for teaching U.S. history: "I want the students to be proud of their cultural differences and to carry those on. We're all different and we need to appreciate each other and be tolerant." Although one teacher seems to focus on similarities and the other on differences, both recognize and use differences.

AFFECTIVE AMBIENCE

Besides awareness and appreciation, there are other affective aspects of the school that relate especially to the international dimension. Helping seems to be expected. The new cafeteria manager says: "I notice kids helping each other. The patrol kids give up part of the lunch hour to sell lunch and those who are bilingual translate for the children who are not yet fluent in English." The school secretary explains that a friend almost always comes to the office with a child who is hurt on the playground.

A new foreign student is usually taken around the school by another child who speaks the same language, if possible. Bilingual students, as well as the teacher who is fluent in Spanish and sometimes bilingual parents, act as translators. In a first grade classroom, a teacher points out a Spanish-speaking student who had been the baby of the class but has suddenly grown up because he has become the interpreter for a new arrival who came from Chile three weeks before. A fifth grade Spanish-speaking girl talks proudly about her responsibility to interpret to the teacher for a new student in her class. In physical education classes the teacher uses a buddy system to make sure directions and rules get translated.

The openness to other languages and interest in helping students extends to American children, too. Thirty percent of the student body participates in the voluntary before-school program in French and Spanish, and, as well, some students are learning from other students. An American boy whose only experience outside the United States is Niagara Falls, Canada, says: "I sit next to a new Spanish-speaking kid. I use my Spanish, but I've been learning very simple Spanish so it sounds like I'm talking primitive to him because he can say 'Hello. I'm well today' and I can only say 'Hello.'" A sixth grade girl who looks forward to traveling but has not been outside the United States says: "It's interesting to have people you're teaching the language [to]. You use sign language sometimes."

The staff is also open to languages other than English. One teacher remembers her own Experiment in International Living experience. "I became very aware of other languages and cultures. I knew how I felt when I wanted to go to the bathroom and couldn't speak. I understand."

The librarian often converses in Spanish with students. One morning, for example, he is talking with a Spanish-speaking kindergartner who is looking for a particular book. A bilingual child who usually speaks only English at school helps out the librarian with the Spanish word for "flying." Says the librarian: "Kids enjoy the fact that you're learning the language. Many of them know more English than I know Spanish. It's not so much the language but the fact you have also learned another language that makes the kids feel better. My two summers in Mexico have made me less sympathetic but more understanding."

The principal often speaks in Spanish to kids in the hall or on the playground, and in his office a child may start a conference in English and end in Spanish and he'll be understanding and try to follow. In a conference with a teacher and a Spanish-speaking parent, the principal will ask the fluent Spanish-speaking teacher to act as interpreter, but his own experience with Italian and Spanish gives him an opportunity to say to the parent, "I know how it is."

SCHOOL REFLECTS COMMUNITY

At Beech Valley, then, both the curriculum and the affective ambience of the school seem to say, "People and things international are okay." Why is this so? The school seems to accept its United Nations characteristics so naturally because the school reflects the community, and the school staff, congruently with the community, seems committed to the "good"—the naturally occurring "good" which rises out of cross-cultural experience.

"The school is a reflection of the community," say several parents. That community is international—at the Y and at the mall, as well as at school. A teacher's aide says: "They live together, too." A teacher points out: "They're neighbors. They socialize. The kids are thrown into this when they're little, and many have traveled, too." Another teacher adds: "It's a healthy thing to have people from many parts of the world living together in a neighborhood, being available in case of emergency."

"My fourth grade son's best friend is Japanese. He loves to eat sushi at his friend's house," says a parent whose family has not been overseas. "A Nigerian family and then a Brazilian family have lived across the street," says another American parent. "That's cross-cultural reinforcement." A third parent notes that her son's best friend was an Australian who moved back to Australia. "They call us and we call them." A fourth parent describes her son's 11th birthday partygoers: a Korean, a Malaysian, an Australian, and two Americans. A Spanish/English bilingual mother is pleased that her son has friends of different religions; he invited his close Jewish friend to his first communion. A Brazilian mother mentions the nationalities of her children's friends (Japanese and Australian and American) who come to their house and learn about different food and games. Still another American parent points out that a number of families in the neighborhood have au pairs to take care of younger children—a Dutch or Danish female, an Asian Indian male.

Of the 19 students interviewed, only one American student said his international contacts were limited to school. Only one Spanish-speaking student who had been in the states less than a year mentioned as friends only other Spanish-speaking students. Otherwise, both American and foreign-born students named students of other nationalities as friends.

"I have a friend who moved back to Brazil," says one American student. "He may not remember me when we're 18 but I liked him a lot." "I've just made friends with someone from Venezuela," says another student. "Two families on my street are from other countries," says a third student. "We play flashlight tag in Spanish sometimes."

A girl who has lived in Kenya and Bangladesh and whose parents are English and Indian lists friends from Bangladesh and Peru. A boy from Malaysia has mostly American friends. A Brazilian girl has friends from Uruguay and the United States as well as Brazil, and a Japanese boy lists friends from the United States, England, Germany, Canada, France, and Switzerland.

The cross-cultural friendships in the neighborhood and at school seem to be generally valued. Although one American parent interviewed says: "I haven't heard parents say 'Oh, isn't it wonderful this school is international,'" some American parents clearly say just that, especially those who have themselves lived overseas. "I love it," "It's exciting," "I'm tickled to death," and "We value a richer environment" are comments from these parents. A parent who has been a leading figure in the International Parents Club because of her experience working with foreign families as she moved around the states with the Army says: "We decided to come back here because of the international community. It's nothing but positive. Basically we get more than we give. People live here because of the international exposure." An American parent who has not lived overseas thinks the international school and community experiences help all the children to become more accepting. "The children don't seem to use nationality as a criterion. Differences are the norm." Another parent says: "When we visited England, friends were afraid our children wouldn't understand the accents, but it was no problem. They were used to different accents."

International parents, too, are generally enthusiastic. A mother who grew up in rural England contrasts her upbringing with that of her children. She saw only similar faces. Her children see all kinds of faces. "They won't have prejudice," she believes, though she admits they don't see economic differences. A Brazilian parent speaks of the school as "opening kids to the universe." A mother from Bangladesh sees the local children becoming more understanding as they are exposed to other cultures. "They see something as custom, not as funny."

Teachers also comment on how the kids get along with each other. A teacher who has been at the school for 23 years and seen the gradual infusion of international people in the last decade describes the school as more cosmopolitan and more democratic than in the past. "We have Moslem, Christian, Jew, Buddhist, Hindu. We've had children from both North and South Vietnam. About the only nationality we haven't had is Russian." She sees the children as generally accepting of each other, and backbiting and namecalling as limited.

Another veteran teacher, of 20 years, also uses the word "accepting" to describe the children. "Occasionally prejudice is expressed," she says, "and we talk about it." She tries to remember an example and tells about a student from Florida who made a disparaging remark about a black boy several years ago.

A younger teacher, who taught in Ohio earlier in her career, says: "The neatest thing is that the American kids are tolerant. Whereas in another school kids might laugh at strange names, they don't laugh here. And they mix."

Students also seem to value the cross-cultural learning opportunities, although only 2 of the 19 interviewed mentioned the international nature of the school when asked to describe it. That question elicited answers about the school programs (specialist teachers), comments about good teachers, and comparisons with other schools (bigger classes than St. Louis, less homework than Malaysia, and not as strict as Brazil).

However, when students were asked what they had learned from being in a school with children of so many different nationalities, they responded as follows:

> You learn things about other countries without teachers, like kids teach games from countries on the playground.
>
> You learn indirectly from kids, from observing, meeting, and talking with them.
>
> You learn how to get along with people.
>
> You learn a lot about different people and how they do things.
>
> It's more fun. It's interesting to learn about other cultures. If you become their friend, they ask you about your experiences or tell you about theirs.
>
> It's good because most kids read in books about kids who are different, like in color, but now that they are mixed up they see that everyone is the same.

A valuing of cross-cultural experience is evident as an American fourth grader who has traveled overseas explains her typology of kids: normal, weird, and interesting. "There are a few normal kids who are American and who just go home and eat dinner and watch TV and do homework and at school get in fights about who goes first in four-square. There are more weird kids who do stuff after school like theater or music. The interesting kids have done something someone else hasn't, like travel somewhere different. I'm halfway between weird and interesting." Her typology corroborates a teacher's observation that foreign kids are perceived by American kids as "more interesting."

There are other salient characteristics of this international community or neighborhood besides the opportunity to live together and have cross-cultural friendships with "interesting" kids. The most important is that this is an affluent community. Although the affluence varies somewhat, as one parent points out, the question is not *whether* but *where* for a vacation. The school has only six families on welfare. One teacher remembers a particular student, the son of a housekeeper in the area, who alone of her students had never been to the Air and Space Museum before the class visit. The students themselves may be conscious of some differences in size of one's house or where one skis, but the fact remains that the community from which the school draws is socioeconomically upper middle class. A mother recalls her daughter's slumber party; race, religion, and nationality differed, but all the fathers were doctors or lawyers.

So socioeconomic class holds constant. There are almost no representatives of what have been defined sociologically and structurally as pariah castes or subordinate minorities, almost no black, Indian, Mexican, or Puerto Rican Americans (Ogbu, 1974, 1978). As one parent points out, "It's easy to be a liberal here." There is a handful of black children, but their parents are at African embassies or from the Caribbean. Besides embassies, foreign parents may be with the World Bank or the International Monetary Fund or the National Defense College. American parents may work for the federal government or teach at American University or be a doctor or lawyer, among other occupations. There are currently one senator and one ambassador among parents. Their children are privileged and have entitlement, an expectation of the class prerogatives of money and power (Coles, 1977).

Related to class are other community characteristics, such as the role of women and the power of parents. Over 95% of the families appear to be two-parent families. Some American mothers work outside the home. Many volunteer at the school. There is a resident artist whose drawings decorate hall walls. A mother who chairs the building and grounds committee spent a fall morning planting bulbs in the front yard of the school. Parents also volunteer in the library, organize the before-school foreign language program, and run the book fair, the auction, and art and hobby night, as well as the mini-course program, the international workshops, and after-school recreation classes such as ballet and cultural arts assemblies. PTA committee chairpersons for the current year include more than 50 different parents. Parent leaders who were interviewed perceived themselves and parents in general as fairly powerful. "Sometimes," said one, "I think parents are running the show." One teacher noted that no teacher who was afraid of demanding parents could teach at Beech Valley.

International parents were not always as involved as American parents. The International Parents Club, under the PTA umbrella, developed as a response to the fact that many foreign mothers did not have the green card enabling them to work and few were active in PTA. Started in 1977 by an English woman, the club now hosts such activities as monthly cooking demonstrations, a Thanksgiving dinner, a fashion show, and a Christmas tea. The group has a welcome kit for new arrivals and also offers American women an opportunity to meet women of other nationalities. Its purpose of providing social activity and acting as a resource for the school—for the International Workshops, for example—seems to have been achieved. The founder quotes a Finnish woman who confided at the end of an International Club coffee, "This has been my best day so far." An American woman, who was an early organizer, notes the support system the club provided for a Japanese woman with a brain tumor. These women acknowledge that their club has not been as successful at reaching out to Latin American women who "tend to socialize among themselves" or to African women "whose husbands don't want their wives to become independent."

Socioeconomic class is also related to the value placed on education by parents and the high expectations they have for their children's performance. "There is academic stress for all," says a teacher's aide. Some teachers modify that generalization to point out that the Chinese and Japanese students seem to be under particular pressure to perform. These students also have their own nationality schools which run all day Saturday. On the other hand, says the teacher, Latin American parents may "shelter their children from the ravages of school." One teacher notes that the image of the country is at stake; thus, all foreign parents want and expect their children to do well at school. Some foreign-born and American children in the neighborhood, perhaps 10%, go to private schools. For example, an American married to an Austrian has enrolled her child in German school because of the language and curriculum which will prepare her daughter to choose between universities in the United States and in Europe.

Good academic performance is particularly valued and obvious at Beech Valley because of a full-time program for fourth through sixth graders who are gifted and a pull-out program for gifted primary pupils. These programs draw both American and foreign-born children. The often-cited example is a Brazilian boy who came to the United States speaking no English and two years later applied for and was accepted in the gifted program. Students in all classes are expected to achieve, however, and the principal points out with some pride that the fifth grade class with the highest scores on the California Achievement Test in the previous year was not the gifted class.

Two final characteristics of the community, related to its international dimension, should be noted. First, the movement of foreign nationals into the community over the last 10 to 20 years has been steady but gradual and pervasive. (As suggested earlier, too, it is not always possible to discern who is a foreign national as opposed to an American citizen of foreign descent or a foreign national who plans a long-term rather than short-term stay in the United States.) There has been a con-current movement of young American families, many also well-traveled, into the area.

A second characteristic of the community is that the foreign nationals are a very diversified group, representing as many as 40 countries from all continents. As several American parents point out, the diversification eliminates a struggle for power or control by one group and probably reduces the tendency to generalize about or stereotype a particular na-tionality. There is no one large minority among the group of foreign families whose children attend Beech Valley.

This international, affluent, well-educated community is now more far-flung than the original neighborhood of the school, which incorpo-rates a gifted program drawing from a district of the school system which was consolidated earlier (after much parent input) with two schools close by. Still, the school seems to be perceived as a neighbor-hood school which reflects the community.

Reflecting an international, affluent, well-educated neighborhood and culture, Beech Valley would be expected to be a school in which the expressed view is that international children are assets and, as one teacher puts it, "the diplomats of the future." In this school the teachers' interaction with children also seems to focus on encouraging internal direction, anticipating the future (especially in regard to work role), and fostering skills in self-presentation—the kind of socialization which has been found in other classrooms of children of professional parents (Wil-cox in Spindler, 1982).

The following statements provide further evidence that the school is congruent with the community in terms of expectations for academic and adult role achievement, and that the school staff, like the leader of the parent groups, are proud of the internationalness of the school:

> We're extremely fortunate because we see kids from all over the world. I try to take advantage of it. We can put a pin in many countries on all con-tinents and say we've experienced them. I want to help the local kids to experience the world vicariously.

> The staff in this school deals with international kids as kids. The impact of the international kids has been very positive.

> The American kids benefit and the foreign families want their children to learn abut the U.S. It's not a one-way thing.

Though the personality of the individual teacher may not be as relevant to understanding this school as the culture of the neighborhood, the experience and commitment of the staff do contribute to the success of the school, again because they are congruent with those of the community members. In this school, class is a commonality for most students, parents, and staff, but beyond that there is a principal and there are teachers who have had cross-cultural experience, as many of the children they teach have had. The empathy, as distinguished from sympathy, that results from cross-cultural experience, is something the staff as a whole seems to possess. Individuals with language experience seem to be particularly empathetic and willing and able to play the role of cultural broker or mediator. Others want to be able to take on that role, such as a teacher who recently transferred into the school and plans to start taking Spanish classes in January, so she can communicate better with some of her first graders. A number of the teachers have been involved in multicultural education courses, and several new teachers speak of looking forward to taking similar courses, which are required by the county, next summer. Such teachers seem concerned about developing intercultural classrooms.

PROBLEMS

Of course, in spite of the expressed and unexpressed goals, and attempts by the staff to be cultural mediators, learning and teaching at Beech Valley are not without difficulties. For example, not everyone gets along all the time. An American boy explains: "No one treats them like we're prejudiced, but sometimes they get abused. When you get mad at someone foreign, you could call them a name. Usually we play together like we're normal though. It's like equal rights."

It is especially hard when one is new and hasn't ever played baseball and isn't sure whether the boy on the block is kidding or not when he says his country is best. So one student who has been in the United States for four months and is learning English says: "I don't like a school with many nationalities. I have friends here but they are different. I had a fight here for some small thing and at home I would never fight." And a Nigerian student says: "I was scared because I was afraid the kids wouldn't like me, but some of the kids here are nice. Some kids say nasty things like, 'fat, ugly, idiot.' Some kids ask 'How come your hair's like that?' and 'How come your mother has marks on her face?' I tell them it makes her look prettier. They even think you have an elephant in your front yard."

It is hard, too, to learn another language, even though it is the perception of most teachers that most students adapt fairly quickly. A Spanish-speaking student says: "Sometimes I cry and I don't want to come to school because I don't speak English so good."

Some teachers admit teaching is a lot harder because of the "language problem." One teacher recognizes the frustration of the Latin American student who was accustomed to being the best student in class but is not here because of her lack of English fluency. She says, "I feel badly when kids aren't understanding for a good part of the day." Teachers have similar methods for dealing with English language learning by foreign students, mostly extra help, patience, grading only the test questions the students understood and passing over the parts he or she didn't. The English as a Second Language teacher praises the staff for being aware of how language develops and being sensitive to individual problems.

Math is universal and thus more comfortable for both the teachers and the foreign students. The specialist teachers in music and art consider their subjects universal, too. In music, singing with words is difficult, but the teacher encourages new students to play instruments, often ones they may be familiar with, like the maracas or guiro from Latin America. She also teaches songs from other countries and asks students to sing songs in their own language.

Beneath the surface, there are some tensions arising from speaking different languages. Occasionally, two kids will be talking in Portuguese and some American kids will think they are being talked about, explains a teacher who is sensitive to that problem. In one class in a previous year, 5 out of 35 students were predominantly Spanish-speakers and the teacher, from his point of view, had to spend too much time with them. Another problem, says a Latin American mother, is that several Spanish-speakers sitting together may not have the incentive to learn English quickly, and parents want their children to learn English. On the other hand, foreign parents also want their children to remember their native language and are not happy if their children speak only English. Some American parents worry about the time the teacher has to spend with non-English-speaking children, too.

As in most schools with a culturally pluralistic population, the basic issue of cultural pluralism versus assimilation exists, even with the acceptance of cultural pluralism as important. On this point, some of the teachers and some of the foreign parents may not agree. A bilingual mother explains how she and her husband have stressed the Latin heritage and urged their children to use and be proud of their bilingualism. Although she values the American experience for her children, a Brazilian mother wants to go home within two more years before her children become too Americanized. A teacher remembers an Iranian mother at a meeting with international parents several years ago who accused the school of changing her son so he didn't want to pray, only to disco. Foreign parents are generally concerned about their children's lack of preparedness for going back home. As children become old enough for junior high and secondary school, the worry about proper education grows. At that point the family may return home so the children can go to school there, or French and German children may go to the schools in those languages in the Washington, D.C. area.

Teachers, on the other hand, say that international students seem to adapt, pick up the language quickly, and want to be like other kids. The teacher may encourage the child to wear a folk costume from his or her country, but the child wants to be Spiderman. Some teachers emphasize the adaptation and say: "It's amazing how they adjust and understand," "Give them a year and they adapt," "One Japanese girl came knowing no English and at the end of the year she had all A's in the sixth grade," and "The child is either assimilated or. . . ."

An American parent points out that the foreign-born children seem to become assimilated and that maybe the opposite happens, too—the American kids become accustomed to children of differing nationalities, religions, and languages. It is certainly true that some American kids learn to love sushi. A fourth grader says matter-of-factly to a friend, "You have more melanin in your skin than I do." A first grader asks a classmate, "You know why Jews don't go to that country?" The differences are accepted and sometimes remarked upon, but more often just accepted.

On a gray November Friday afternoon when 75 students in the intermediate gifted program are crowded in one classroom watching Bill Cosby in the film "On Prejudice," intercultural awareness and acceptance seem obvious. The students are visibly uncomfortable during the 20 minutes of unrelieved bigotry. At one point an American boy puts his arm around the Japanese boy sitting next to him on a desk top. The students discuss the film afterward; they seem united against the bigotry Cosby portrays in the film, putting down every group represented in the room in harsh, stereotypic generalizations. But the teacher has shown the film to point up another kind of prejudice, prejudice against students who are in the gifted program and prejudice against students who are not. "How," asks the teacher, "can we make things better so that there won't be prejudice against the gifted program?" A student says: "Could we have more activities with other classes? I don't see my friends from before very often." The teacher asks for more ideas to be brought in on Monday. Then it is time for recess.

So this "little United Nations" school where internationalism is natural still struggles with prejudice, albeit a different kind. The fact that the struggling is done with student involvement is significant and sets the picture of the school in a wider frame. For Beech Valley does not advertise itself as a little United Nations school or as an international school.

The principal and teachers and parents and children think of it first as a good school. The principal said as much in his message to parents in the summer PTA bulletin.

> In the recent studies I've read, the same characteristics are stressed when defining a good school. High academic achievement, democratic procedures, warm cooperative spirit, and constant feedback among others are present in each good school. Sound familiar? I believe so—for these are characteristics which I found at Beech Valley and which the staff and I continue to nourish.

Beech Valley is a good school whose neighborhood happens to be international and whose staff has also had international experiences. The congruence works. The focus on characteristics of a "good school" works. It's a natural!

Chapter 7

International Student Visitors at School: "Someone from Another World"

Traveling on the new, straight, wide-cut section of a road in southeastern Ohio, one notes a historical marker advertising a mine disaster site of 50 years ago. Then the two-lane state highway returns to hug a cliff, then wends its way through three small towns strung along in a row. At the third town, the highway, a creek, and a railroad wind together through the long, narrow town. The several blocks of storefronts include a Krogers, a funeral home, a dress shop, and several bars. Some storefronts are empty. There are also several gas stations. Across the railroad tracks at the one traffic light, left on a bumpy brick street, and around the corner, across from a little white-frame United Mthodist church, is the school—a very different school from Beech Valley.

Bright red doors cheer the old two-story building, which was a high school until 1972. It is now Cornwall Middle School, housing the fifth, sixth, seventh, and eighth graders of a 1,300 pupil district. Kindergarten through fourth grade and high school classes occupy a new, open-space building in the neighboring town.

The principal isn't sure whether the school district is the poorest or the next-to-the-poorest in the state of Ohio. Sixty percent of the students get a free lunch. Adults of the community work as miners (driving to another county), as custodians (perhaps in the university which is 15 miles away), or as farmers; when they can get work, often they hold several jobs. There are many single parents. The children want to be truck drivers and miners and nurses; one student talked about wanting a job that would pay good money, like a schoolteacher. Perhaps 5% of the district's graduates go on to college, almost all to the nearby regional state university. The principal speaks proudly of the school system's alumnus at Harvard. Someone else from the district holds a football scholarship in Kansas.

One rainy autumn day in Cornwall's basement art room, 13 fifth graders are watching slides of Brazil and listening to Andrea, a Brazilian student of International Studies at the nearby regional state university. Andrea is a vivacious brunette dressed in a red blouse, tight black pants, and boots. She shows a slide of São Paulo and announces: "This is my city." "How many times did you change planes to come here?" someone asks. She answers and then shows a slide with a map of Brazil showing different regions. She describes the next slides. "See how many rivers we have. Look how many flowers we have." Her voice sings as she speaks. "The south is cold, the opposite of this country." The students seem interested in her explanation of summer being winter and winter being summer in Brazil, but when she asks "Who likes soccer?" their involvement is complete. Almost all the students raise their hands. Several have heard of Pele. Several others describe the differences between soccer and football.

These boys and girls and Andrea are part of a special outreach Cultural Awareness Project of the local university. With some 1,500 foreign students from 90 countries, the university is a rich resource for this most racially homogeneous and most culturally isolated region of Ohio. In connection with this project, originally funded by the National Endowment for the Humanities, international students from Brazil, Indonesia, and Nigeria (nations chosen by the teachers of the first schools involved in the project) have helped develop artifact kits, have been involved in workshops for teachers, and have made many classroom visits.

The following case study looks at the impact of the visitors on one school. The question is: Can visits by international students and interaction with the materials they bring (slides, books, musical instruments, clothes, games) be a stimulating substitute for the absence of cross-culturally experienced teachers and students in a school? Since students had participated in the program over several years, they (including seventh graders not currently part of the program) were asked about past as well as current visitors.

WHAT THE STUDENTS SAY

After an analysis of student interviews and papers, four points stand out relative to impact on students. (1) In talking and writing about both what they had learned recently and what they remembered from previous years, students most often mentioned artifacts used by the international visitor. (2) Some students seemed to focus on differences between cultures and "weirdness." (3) But most students would like to travel to the home countries of the international visitors. (4) All students agreed the project was a good idea, most because they "learned more"— a point made by the students in the classes of Michael and Angela in chapter 3.

As students talked about what they had learned, clothes ranked first in student interest and memory. Fifth graders said: "The clothes were neat" and "The clothes were fantastic." Sixth graders remembered clothes from their fifth grade experience with Nigeria. One boy proudly recalled that his teacher had taken a picture of him "dressed up." Another boy recalled others trying on clothes, but said he didn't want to. A third boy remembered the clothes the Nigerian visitor had worn as "kinda silk." Talking about their current Indonesian experience, sixth graders were enthusiastic about trying on hats. Some seventh graders, no longer part of the program, recalled trying on Nigerian clothes in fifth grade and Indonesian hats in sixth. "They brought nice clothes," said one.

Students also recalled music, games, puppets, and language. They described Nigerian musical instruments, games from both Nigeria and Indonesia, Indonesian puppets, and a little language learning. Comments included: "I really liked the drums"; "He had a record and we danced to it"; "They showed us how to play a game and we made one from an egg carton"; "I liked the way the puppets moved"; and "We learned how to say good-by in Yoruba."

Memories of the Brazilian visitors and artifacts were much less frequently mentioned, perhaps because that experience is part of the art class and not common to all students. Five of the twenty sixth graders and one of fourteen seventh graders interviewed had no memories to share of their experiences a year or two years before.

Some students, particularly fifth graders, seemed especially conscious of differences between Americans and the cultures represented by the guests. For example, asked to write what they had learned about Nigeria, 10 (or half) of the fifth graders in one class used the word "different" at least once. Wrote one girl: "What they wore was so much different they tie their cloth around their waist instead of zipping or buttoning it." A boy's three sentence paragraph stated that money, clothes, and language were different. Other students mentioned schools, religion, homes, and roads as being different. One student said Nigerians look different and another noted that they carried their bodies differently. The following is an example of a complete paragraph in which one fifth grader focuses on differences:

I thought her clothing was differnt and her food. And they have differnt homes than ours. Then the differnt money then ours and change. And she's got differnt hair. And there babies have to have there ears pearsed when there born. And there bicycles are not too high. And they have differnt language and differnt shoes.

It is not surprising, of course, that some students seemed so aware of the differences. One boy remarked that the Nigerian and Brazilian guests were the first foreigners he had ever met; he noticed their strong accents. Another student wrote in a thank-you letter: "It seemed funny for a Nigeria lady to come down, but I guess I just am not used to people from other countries, states, or colonies to come down." Even a student who seemed more knowledgeable than most about the world (he recognized that the Nigerian visitor spoke English as well as Yoruba and he talked about "meeting a guy from Italy at Grandpa's house" whom he couldn't understand) noted that before, he had always thought of just jungles in connection with Africa.

A fifth grade girl, trying to sort out what she had learned and how she felt about it, described the musical instruments as "weird." The visitor was "hard to understand" but the "way she talked was interesting" and "she was pretty." Several other fifth grade girls seemed especially willing to change previously held ideas: "I didn't think they had cars and I learned they did. I thought they might wear weird clothes but they weren't that weird." "Before, I knew Tarzan movies but I learned about the clothes and how the music was. I didn't know before." Another girl, in her letter to the Nigerian guest, wrote: "Thank you for being patient with us and using your time to help us understand everything about Africa better. I will give you my address and maybe me and your girl can be pen pals."

Sixth and seventh graders used the words "different" and "weird" occasionally in their papers or in conversation. A sixth grader wrote in his Indonesian "book": "The hats are very weird." Another wrote: "There music is funny there words are spelled funny and they writing is funny." Generally, however, the sixth grade "books" on Indonesia dealt fairly straight forwardly with a variety of topics, from weather and products (probably the result of textbook or encyclopedia forays) to shadow puppets and kitchen utensils which are part of the kits. Their "books" also included a map and sometimes a song and a spice chart. One wonders about the sources of some written generalizations such as "Indonesia has very hot weather and it is so jambed up that it makes it hotter than it already is" and "The Indonesian people use bow and arrows, stone hatches and knives for hunting."

The picture of Indonesia students shared in interviews seemed more accurate and more reflective of the Indonesian student's visit and interaction with kit materials. One especially talkative sixth grader recognized that both Indonesia and Nigeria are "kinda modern." He knew there were both rich and poor people in these countries and compared Indonesian and Nigerian clothes. However, he also talked about "monkeys jumping from building to building" in Nigeria.

Several seventh graders remembered "different" games and language. One girl began by talking about "weird clothes" and "different accents" and said she wouldn't want to visit a country with weirdos," but later in the conversation, as she talked about why the program was pretty good" she indicated more openness and a capacity to see various perspectives. "How we live is weird for them," she said, "and it's neat to learn how they live . . . We complain and they beg to go to school . . . Some people here are down on black people and discriminate . . . There are Nigerians in our church and they bring food that looks awful to potluck but it tastes good. It's interesting the way they talk, too." This student was beginning to see Americans as weird and Nigerians as interesting as well as vice versa. At the end of the interview, she said, "It might be interesting to go to their country for a week and see all the things."

Her change of mind meant that all the seventh graders agreed they would like to visit the home countries of their guests. One boy was especially enthusiastic. "I'd like to visit all those foreign countries for the experience. I'd like to go learn how they talk." In contrast to most of the students, however, he probably saw such travel a very possible because his brother is in the Army in Frankfurt, Germany. The sixth graders were more hestitant about traveling to another country: 11 said yes, 5 were unsure, and 4 said no. But the fifth graders were adventuresome; only 2 out of 26 didn't want to visit Nigeria.

The Cornwall students interviewed were not untraveled, but they were limited in their travel experience. Out of 60 students, 14 had been to Florida. Only 7 never had been out of Ohio, but West Virginia, close by, was the out-of-state travel mentioned by 12 students. One student had lived in Florida, one in Mississippi, one in Maryland, and one in California. One fifth grader talked knowledgeably about her trip to Williamsburg, Virginia; another described the places his truck driver father had traveled, and still another listed 10 states she had visited and said it made her sick to go up and down in the mountains. One sixth grader had visited his aunt in the Army in Kentucky, another had gone to the Grand Canyon, but there was also a sixth grader who remembered going once to the other side of Columbus, less than 100 miles away. No one mentioned having flown in an airplane; in fact, several mentioned not wanting to fly as a reason for not wanting to visit another country.

While most students said they would like to visit the home countries of their international visitors, the question may not have seemed like a real one, and the "yea, sure" was casual and perhaps not quite believing. For those who were reluctant about overseas travel, the countries just seemed too far away and some worried about different language and food.

The reluctant travelers, however, were in agreement with all the other students that the program bringing international students to Cornwall was a good idea. Students answered the follow-up "why" matter-of-factly in a number of ways, but more than half said that they "learned more." A sample of responses includes:

> You learn more because it's the real thing.
>
> You wouldn't learn too much from a book.
>
> Because when you get older you may want to travel and you'd know stuff about their country before you got there.
>
> So they know about our stuff and get to know us.
>
> You can see what they really look like and how they talk.
>
> So if they come we could understand them a little better.
>
> Cause they come in and learn you stuff about the way they live. The real person's there to make you understand better.
>
> Because we can learn more about other countries and it will help us in social studies.
>
> The person knows more about it than the teacher.
>
> They can show you stuff and the book don't.
>
> With someone telling us it seems like you can ask questions and he can give reasons.
>
> We don't learn that much in social studies about them and we wouldn't be able to do our reports.
>
> People can tell you.
>
> It was more exciting.
>
> In case we move there.

Beyond answering simply "We learned more," then, a number of students saw the advantages of the real persons as resources to "tell" them about their countries, to answer their questions, to help them understand, to help them in social studies. Some students thought the new knowledge would be helpful if they ever went to Nigeria or Indonesia. And some students recognized the program was fun!

WHAT THE TEACHERS AND PRINCIPAL SAY

The three teachers who volunteered to participate in the Cultural Awareness Project are somewhat different in personal backgrounds and in how they build curriculum around the visits. The impact of the program on them personally differs, too, but they have in common strongly stated beliefs about its significance for students. The principal and some of the other teachers share those beliefs.

The art teacher was a northern Ohio city girl who grew up and decided to live in the country near a college town. She finds it interesting to get to know someone from another culture and to compare and contrast cultures. She notices her pupils doing some comparing, too: "the Statue of Liberty to the statue of Christ in Rio," and McDonalds here and there. Before her Brazilian guest came, she showed a movie about a Brazilian family, and after the visits she usually plans a related art project. Felt birds and carnival masks were previous projects. This year she wasn't sure she would have time for a project because Halloween was the next week.

The fifth grade teacher also grew up in an Ohio city, Dayton. An exchange student from Mexico lived with her family when she was a teenager, but she had never had contact with anyone black. Now, after working with three different Nigerian visitors in the last three years, she feels more comfortable with the Nigerians than with African-Americans. "My cognitive learning has also been great," she reports. "I didn't know the capital or leader or about the grassy plains or all that oil." With her class, she has concentrated on communication skills, and combined language arts and social studies in the study of Nigeria. She starts with some map study, gives her students some historical background, spends several days on folk tales, and includes an Africa puzzle and an art project. She stresses that Africa is not all jungle or all poor. When a student asked if the prospective visitor was a "nigger," she explained why that word should not be used.

The sixth grade teacher is from the Cincinnati area and went to college in Kentucky and Chicago before coming to southeastern Ohio with her husband who was doing graduate work. Like the fifth grade teacher, this is her eleventh year at Cornwall, but unlike the fifth grade teacher and art teacher she lives in the university town and claims there is a 75-year culture lag between the town where the school is located and the university town. She has been to Europe twice and in every state east of Kansas, and her family has hosted international students. Skirting the question of personal impact of the program, she describes various activities for her unit on Indonesia, including a spice chart and an international linkages lesson from materials developed by the project. She uses Indonesian books for her reading class and teaches her students Indonesian greetings. She is especially interested in using the kits of artifacts.

The three teachers agree on their perceptions of the program's significance for the students. Says the fifth grade teacher: "It's good for them. They gain a realization that the world doesn't end at Ohio's borders or the Atlantic Ocean." She got into the project because "it sounded interesting and I just felt the kids were deprived. They have no concept of anything beyond blue jeans and video games." The sixth grade teacher comments: "The program alerted students to the fact there is a world out there. It's the best program brought into the schools, bar none." Beyond this general awareness of the world and other peoples, which the art teacher also mentions, the three teachers have noticed students picking up on commonalties and developing a tolerance for differences. "They no longer make fun of differences," says the sixth grade teacher. "It's okay to be different." This learning seems important to her in view of the differences in socioeconomic class and antagonism among the small towns which the children experience. The fifth grade teacher thinks the students learned that differences in color or in lifestyles don't mean inferiority. She also points out, however, that "kids get a deeper appreciation of their own country."

The teachers most supportive of the program are the other fifth and sixth grade teachers, who see the visitors and observe their students' responses, and the librarian. "The children liked comparing their names in Portuguese," says one. "The personal contact helps them understand," says another. "The people are not as different as they imagined." The librarian notes that the students seem "to get excited about the people, especially when they bring things." Students check out books, too. She has about 100 books, including some duplicates, which are about other countries, most published in the 1960s and 1970s, some series like *My Village* and *Let's Travel*. If the students can't find an appropriate book, she directs them to the encyclopedia; the most recent one is four years old.

In contrast to the fifth grade teacher who reported that seventh graders hadn't forgotten their Nigerian guest and talked about wanting to visit her, the seventh and eighth grade teachers did not see much lasting impact of the program. The language arts teacher says: "It hasn't ever come up in their journals." The reading teacher says: "The program hasn't come up in discussions and they usually talk about things if they are really interested. The eighth graders just had a story on South Africa."

The social studies teacher says the students talked about the visitors (several seventh graders called one international visitor by name during the interviews) but couldn't identify the country they were from. "They could describe things brought in and what the person wore." He concludes that the visual aspect was what was retained. Although one of his stated goals is to open the students' eyes and show there is something beyond their small town, his tactics do not necessarily complement and follow up the students' experience with the international visitors through the Cultural Awareness Project. Talking about showing his slides of his Mexican honeymoon, for instance, he says that students would "see a school that's worse than ours and would remember the kids with bloated stomachs." Although seventh grade geography is more physical than cultural, he is committed to current events discussions and has taken graduate courses on China, Japan, and the former Soviet Union.

The principal is convinced of the program's worth. A young, energetic idea-seeker and implementer, he is obviously proud of his school's progress on tests and a new discipline program, but he is concerned about curriculum as well. One reason for his openness to the Cultural Awareness Project may be his own cross-cultural experience in Korea with the Army. "It made me more empathetic, appreciative." He also credits his religious belief in one world with all people under God. In talking about the program he says: "Anything that shows how we're part of one world is important. What I want out of this is that students realize that their life may not be here and even if it is, decisions they make will affect the world. We want our students not just to be successful in the district and nation but also the world." He sees both teachers and students becoming increasingly involved in the project. "At $30.00 the program is a bargain," he concludes.

So he and the fifth and sixth grade teachers and the art teacher agree on the significance of the program for Cornwall: to open students' eyes to the world and to help them learn to accept differences. The awareness and tolerance they want their students to gain seems to be developing. Although student written and oral responses were most often specific and cognitive ("They carry stuff on their head"), there were students who responded to the person ("I remember Joshua" and "The Indonesian man was nice and sweet") and some who were beginning to think about what differences in people and cultures might mean and to accept them ("Her hair was different and pretty").

WHAT INTERNATIONAL VISITORS SAY

The international student visitors participating in the program reacted to several parts of the experience in interviews: the school situation itself, their own participation, and rationales for the program. Three spoke about their recent visits to Cornwall; the fourth and fifth added perspectives from other years and other schools.

The Cornwall School situation was a surprise, perhaps even a shock to the visitors. Andrea, who had been a high school exchange student in Indianapolis before working on an International Studies university degree, explains that this, her second round as an international visitor, was completely different. "Such a poor school," she says. "Such a huge, developed country to have such schools." It is her perception that the teacher was having a difficult time motivating the students. "The children have a lot of potential, but they have everything on television and it takes a lot of creativity to motivate them." Besides showing slides, she had made candy, played games with the class, and brought in magazines and money. She also translated all the students' names into Portuguese. "I pretend I know a translation even if I don't."

To Syarif, an Indonesian television commentator at home, Cornwall School also seemed poor: "We have nicer schools in Indonesia." He also points out that in Indonesia children are expected to respect adults. During his first visit to Cornwall, he was surprised at the number of students who didn't pay attention and the teacher's lack of control. Ironically, the teacher was sitting at her desk working on discipline posters. To the Indonesian visitor, it seemed as though the teacher was looking down on someone from another country by going on with her work. "People here don't realize the status of international students at home," he suggests. "Many are directors of agencies." Certainly the class and status of the international visitors did conflict with the situation at Cornwall. One of the other international participants explained that he had come to realize, through his encounter with rural schools in the "less developed" United States, that he was out of touch with that part of his own country's population.

The third visitor's reactions show that the teacher's involvement with the class and the visitor is critical for the overall success of the visit. Deborah, from Nigeria, although noting she had never thought any place in the United States would not be beautiful, has only positive things to say about the children and the teacher. "I enjoyed them. I didn't want to leave that last Friday. And the teacher was so good to me." She smiles and laughs as she reads her thank-you letters. "I'm so happy. I love those kids." She is especially interested in the child who wanted to be her daughter's pen pal.

Deborah patiently answered questions during the first visit. "I expected those silly questions," she says, "but they should know we have cars and motorcycles. Eventually they knew there's not much difference in some things." She was impressed that the teacher had taught the game of ayo. During later visits she played Sunny Ade's music, dressed up the children, and wrote numbers in Yoruba.

For Syarif, the third visit, during which his wife and a friend taught a children's game, seemed more successful than the first visit with slides and endless questions about whether Indonesia has cars and telephones. "I didn't tell them we had the fourth communications satellite." He didn't feel the students had learned much before he came, although the teacher had taught them to say "Welcome" in Indonesian. But "teachers asked questions that made me realize they don't know much about the rest of the world," he says. He compares the American and

Indonesian curricula. "In third grade I knew the capital of Peru and the president of the United States."

The students had lots of questions for Andrea, too. "They don't know we have TV!" She told the classes that Brazilians wear jeans like Americans. "For me, teaching was easy," she says. "I've done it before and I like children." That was obvious as she related weather, food, and football to the class's experience and praised a fifth grader who knew about the Amazon River.

Participation in the Cultural Awareness Project seemed to reinforce the international students' commitment to helping Americans learn about the rest of the world. "I would like to do it again," say both first-timers. "It's a beautiful thing," says Deborah, "to get people who are actually from there." Said another Nigerian, a member of the project in the previous year, "The most important part is for the children to learn to do away with some of their misconceptions." He told them about his son who is an airplane pilot. Another participant from a previous year, a newcomer to the United States shocked by the "abject lack of knowledge," summed up the importance of the project: "It is a thrill to know about another place. This is a good program and needed now and in the future as the world grows smaller."

CONCLUSIONS

In a school in which there are teachers and students who represent cultural differences, an international student resource program may be enrichment. A Beech Valley mother bringing Swedish bread to a third grade which includes students from eight different countries and is taught by a teacher who has lived in Japan, Panama, and Germany may be tasty frosting on an already rich and multilayered cake. But at Cornwall and other isolated rural schools, the task of inspiring cultural awareness is more basic. Such a program as the Cultural Awareness Project may be likened to yeast which will stimulate the rising of the bread of everyday experience.

The Cultural Awareness Project has made a difference for some Cornwall students and teachers. It can continue to do so, although it will probably be difficult to quantify the difference and difficult to be sure how the project will contribute to decision-making from a global perspective by a future citizen who was once a Cornwall student. Perhaps it is enough to begin with the plain good feeling the project has produced. As one student, asked why he like the program, replied: "It's just nice to have someone from another world around."

Chapter 8

The International Studies Academy: Becoming an International Educational Community

Schools may take advantage of their internationally experienced population, as Beech Valley Elementary did and still does. They may import internationally experienced people to broaden the horizons of their students through a special university program, as Cornwall Middle School did. They may also decide to "become international," as Washington High School's magnet program, the International Studies Academy, did. The original case study description, based on observation and interviews done over the school year 1984-85, is augmented by data gathered in September 1992 through follow-up interviews with the woman who had been Washington High's associate principal in charge of the International Studies Academy and who became principal in August 1992, and with one of the teachers who became the director of the International Baccalaureate Program of the Academy the year after the original research was completed.

As for many other urban international magnet programs, the basic *raison d'être* for Washington's International Studies Academy was desegregation. In 1984-85, as it is presently, a challenging college preparatory curriculum was the most widely advertised and generally agreed upon goal of the program, perhaps because of some teachers' involvement in a Traditional Academic Program, and with advanced placement courses, and then with the International Baccalaureate—and also because rigor and excellence are demanded by the public. And yet the

Academy, and some would say the whole school, is in the process of becoming international. An English as a Second Language Program, serving all the high school students who need it (about 75 in 1984-85 and about 120 in 1992-93), adds mostly Asian (in 1984-85) as well as eastern European immigrants (by 1992) to the African-American/Anglo-American mix of students.

International experience is an asset for faculty already in the school, such as a returned Peace Corps volunteer from Malaysia. It is considered an asset for new faculty, such as a woman who taught for 10 years in Kenya, and is sought after by other faculty members, such as a teacher with a summer Fulbright award to India. An English teacher adds the Nigerian writer Chinua Achebe to the curriculum, and a social studies teacher asks students to interview foreign-born persons for a U.S. history project. The foreign language classes read their own poetry in Spanish, French, and German at a special Mother's Day assembly which Chinese, Dutch, and Spanish visitors attend. Some students take International Baccalaureate exams for a course of study headquartered in Geneva, Switzerland.

This case study describes the International Studies Academy and its home high school, Washington. It includes goals, highlights and disappointments, and life in classrooms and at several special events during one school year, 1984-85. It looks especially at the ways in which the Academy was attempting to "become international" and at issues the Academy was addressing at that time. It explains what happened to some of the dreams faculty and administrators expressed and concludes with the new principal's dreams for the future.

The possiibility that schools can respond to having internationalness thrust upon them and become international is important because it means schools can take leadership in preparing students for life in a globally interdependent world. To ask whether American education should be globalized is a nonsensical question (Anderson, 1982). However, how that global education will happen and how schools will become internationalized are valid questions. Global or international education can happen through individual teacher efforts such as those by Angela or Michael, or it can happen through a structural change, as at Washington High School. Teachers may change schools, but schools may also change teachers. This study describes how one magnet program at one school is trying to change people—teachers and students—in an attempt to become international.

THE ISA IN WASHINGTON HIGH SCHOOL

The International Studies Academy (ISA) is a school-within-a-school which draws students from all over the city and from private and suburban schools. (Note that the present tense will be used to describe 1984-85 at the ISA and changes since 1985 will be added parenthetically.) The ISA has three divisions which occasionally overlap for individual students. The International Program (now called the World Awareness Program), an international studies curriculum designed for the average and above average student, provides a natural extension of the elementary and middle school bilingual program and allows for continuous foreign language instruction through grade 12. The K–8 foreign language program allows students to receive 25% to 50% of their instruction in French, Spanish, or German (by 1992 Arabic, Chinese, Japanese, and Russian had been added.) Besides providing an opportunity to continue a foreign language (or to start one if the student comes from a school which is not part of the bilingual program), the International Program encourages students to take four years of English, three or four years of social studies and math, the interdisciplinary course "The Human Condition," and physical education and health.

The International Baccalaureate Program is more rigorous than the International Program. The IB, as it is known, consists of six basic subject areas plus three additional requirements. Generally, three subject areas are studied for two years (high level) and three subject areas are studied for one year (subsidiary level). The IB curriculum provides students with a comprehensive background in English, a foreign language, the social sciences, physical and life sciences, mathematics, and the arts. Additional requirements include a course in the theory of knowledge, a 5,000 word essay in one of the six subject areas, and artistic, creative, or social service activity. The International Baccalaureate Organization in Geneva, Switzerland is responsible for the preparation and grading of all IB external examinations and for program review and the awarding of diplomas and certificates. The IB diploma is accepted at many foreign universities and at American colleges, where full first year standing is often granted. Most IB students at Washington are certificate candidates who sit for examinations in their strongest subjects, prepare an essay, and participate in a social service activity. These students typically take some courses in the regular International Program as well. In 1985, 56 students took IB exams; 6 students took the full diploma, and 1 student got the full diploma. (In 1992, 85 students took IB exams.)

The third program in the ISA is English as a Second Language (ESL), designed for foreign-born students who have limited English proficiency. As the students acquire English proficiency, they begin taking classes in the International Program or the International Baccalaureate or in the comprehensive or vocational programs also available at Washington High School. Most of the ESL students are refugees, and most of the refugees were from Cambodia in 1985, but other countries represented included Afghanistan, China, Ethiopia, Greece, Iran, Israel, Jamaica, and Vietnam. In the IB program there were students from France, India, Sri Lanka, and Vietnam. Three teachers teach not only English as a Second Language but also survival skills and some social studies.

Although the ISA claims about one-fourth of Washington's students, it is not an obviously separate school-within-a-school to a person walking into Washington. It does have a separate office for the associate principal, the coordinator, and the counselor who are administrators for the program. The ISA is separate for the purposes of discipline and counseling, although the counselor spent the last quarter of the school year 1984-85 filling in for another counselor who had moved to another job. ISA teachers are connected to the rest of the school by the fact that most of them teach comprehensive classes as well as ISA classes. ISA students are connected to the rest of the school through their participation in school activities; they play in the band and play football, they run track and run for Prom Queen, they are class officers and club members.

Washington High School has a history which is still evident to students and teachers, especially in the building and grounds. Built in 1919 on 27 acres, Washington is an impressive place, distinguished by, as the alma mater states, "gentle slopes and lofty tower, arching bridge and shaded valley." Inscribed on a wall of the tower is "Let all who will enter find within these walls equal and varied opportunity for a liberal education." The school opened with two swimming pools, three gyms, a stadium seating 8,000 people, and a large pipe organ. In 1985, although deemed in need of major and minor repair by a recent accreditation team, the physical plant was adequate. The vocational wing, cafeteria, some classrooms, and a mini-auditorium were fairly new.

The Washington Tower inscription was transposed into the slogans "Something for everyone . . . the best for the most" and "the most comprehensive high school in the state." Indeed, the accreditation team mentioned Washington's reputation as one of the most comprehensive high schools in the nation. One hundred teachers teach 200 courses. The approximately 2,000 students have vocational opportunities in art, business, home economics, horticulture, and trade and industry, as well as regular comprehensive classes in basic subjects and college preparation possibilities in the International Studies Academy. An issue of the *Tower News* publicized the facts that the Nurses' Aide Program had 100% job placement for the sixth year, cosmetology students provided volunteer services to an average of 25 patients a week at a local hospital, the construction electricity classes completed 35 wiring jobs both in and out of school, and the graphic arts students helped local businesses and community groups with art work. Over 450 students participated in vocational clubs.

The perception of some outsiders is that Washington is a poor, black school. That is somewhat accurate; the International Studies Academy is one of a number of magnet programs which are part of the school system's desegregation effort. Statistics show that 46% of Washington's students were classified as low income and 72.6% black in the fall of 1984. The perception is one the ISA has to deal with as it recruits students. In the spring of 1985 about 200 black students were still in line for places in the ISA, but they could be accepted only as more white students were accepted. Applications had come, however, from a prestigious private school and from Catholic schools. Racial statistics for the ISA in 1984-85 were 55% black, 30% white, and 15% other, primarily Asian, but most students in the IB classes are black. There are other ways to describe Washington's varied student body: guys and gals wearing jeans and polo shirts, but a girl with purple tennis shoes and green socks and a boy wearing one earring and a girl in a white uniform also stand around Washington Tower at lunch.

Part of the reality about Washington seems to be that there is a new pride. Teachers who are old hands at the school explain that the ISA has elevated the whole school, given it a shot in the arm, maybe even a new identity. More books are carried now than radios or ghettobusters. A comprehensive class asks to write research papers. "There was a time when eggheads were looked down upon. Now it is cool to learn," says one teacher. Another notes more seriousness about studying, but does not think the ISA students are stimulating other students very much. The ISA students have undeniably given new life to some co-curricular activities. In 1984-85, student announcers, 60% of the band, two-thirds of the swim team, and most of the soccer team were ISA students.

Getting the reality of the ISA and Washington understood in the community is a tough job. The person responsible for the *Tower News*, which is sent to parents and the community, wishes that the ISA would get more credit for what is it doing. Instead of Washington, for example, a chief rival school for outstanding students which has a long established college preparatory program gets mentioned in a state publication. Using that rival school as a yardstick is not infrequent among faculty. An ISA teacher who is a graduate of the rival school says that the IB program is tougher, but teachers who wish for higher caliber students blame the rival school for continuing to take the top students in the city. (Several years later, a center with five more magnet programs opened, increasing the competition.) On the other hand, several teachers whose own children attend or have attended the rival school have not seriously considered Washington as an alternative. Using the other school as a yardstick is inevitable since one of the ISA's goals is to provide a challenging college preparatory program, but it detracts from the international perspective goal, which to some is already secondary. The question of identity will be raised again, in relation to goals and outcomes, as well as in terms of the relationship of the ISA to Washington High School itself.

GOALS, HIGHLIGHTS, AND DISAPPOINTMENTS

It is an August morning and entering freshmen and their parents are filling the mini-auditorium, listening to administrators explain and inspire, waiting for students to take them on a tour of the two and one-half miles of high school corridors. The associate principal who directs ISA describes learning as discovering that all things are possible and that schools are places of struggle and growth. She asks students to hitch their wagons to a star. The IB coordinator talks about trying to develop an educational community. He says the focus will be on the student—on college preparation, on communication skills, and on providing students with an international view and exposing them to other cultures. The counselor asks, "What are you going to do with your life?" she says, "You are in the process of becoming and that is your job."

Becoming what? The *Tower News* answers that question. "The International Studies Academy is a unique program designed to prepare 9th, 10th, 11th and 12th graders for an active role as world citizens through a challenging curriculum of academics, critical thinking, and problem solving." The poster by the office door bears the slogan "World leadership begins in the classroom."

These are the public and public relations goals, but how do administrators, teachers, and students see the purposes of the ISA? Both in public and private, the associate principal describes her goal as a strong international studies program. At a reception for International Baccalaureate students, she states:

> Many of us are not even aware how closely our communities are linked with other countries and cultures, although the fortieth anniversary of Hiroshima, the tragedies of Ethiopia and South Africa, and our concerns about nuclear disarmament have certainly directed our attention to this reality. We must begin to understand that though we are citizens of the United States, we are also residents of the Earth, and, as such, have certain responsibilities for understanding the complex problems of the world and for contributing to the betterment of the world community. Certainly this is the primary goal of the ISA—to increase our students' awareness of the world, to create within them a sense of world responsibilities and global values.

Although proud of the IB students, the associate principal is not as concerned about number and pass rates in the IB as she is about what is best for the individual student, not only in IB but in the whole program.

The IB coordinator believes the program must be sold to parents and students as college preparation, although he also believes development of an international perspective is critical. The counselor and several faculty members mention only academic excellence when asked what they believe the goals of the ISA are. For example, one teacher sees the goals as to better prepare young people for college and to fill them with a desire to learn. Most teachers talk about the twin goals of promoting intellectual excellence and an international perspective. Says one: "We want to build students' perceptions of themselves as part of the world community and we want to meet the challenges the kids bring and challenge them and us." Says another: "We want to promote intellectual, intercontinental experiences." Sometimes teachers rank their goals, as does one who emphasizes academics first but thinks a very important secondary goal is promoting cultural awareness and understanding. For her, the intercultural aspect involves not only learning about other cultures, but also promoting better human relations between blacks and whites and with new arrivals like the Cambodian refugees. One teacher speaks earnestly about believing that we need to teach relationship to others if we are going to survive as a species. "We can use our brains to reach out and touch each other. We can start with the intellect and learn how people are both the same and different." Says a language teacher who expects greater proficiency from her students: "I want us to pull ourselves out of ethnocentrism."

Interviews with nine students reveal that some students see the goals of the ISA as mostly academic and some see the goals as both academic excellence and gaining an international perspective. A freshman says the main goals are to introduce foreign students to American traditions and American students to foreign cultures and to offer a better education. A sophomore says that the ISA gives you a more international point of view and makes you able to compete in a shrinking world. A senior mentions both a global perspective and college preparation. A student who grew up in France believes the ISA offers a broader view of the world than the suburban school she attended previously. The other five students do not mention an international perspective as a goal until specifically asked how the ISA prepared them for world leadership. A better education is their primary concern, though one student recognizes that the IB program will enable her to go to college anywhere in the world and another points out that a better education should include a world perspective.

A look at the connection between goals stated at the beginning of the year and highlights and disappointments shared at the end of the school year is instructive. For the IB coordinator and the counselor the highlights are student achievement, matching their goals. Says the coordinator: "I could hug all the students who took the IB exam." The counselor is disappointed with the SAT scores. The coordinator also wishes for more internationalization of the international program curriculum, in line with his concern for an international perspective. The associate principal's list of highlights includes special events such as the International Club Dinner and the achievements of teachers selected to be Fulbright participants; a disappointment relates to a particular student. The associate principal's goal of a strong international studies program is not as tied up with the International Baccalaureate; her concern is for the total program.

For IB teachers, however, particularly at the end of the year and soon after reading the exams, the highlights and disappointments are often directly related to the IB program and the exams. For example, two teachers who listed only international perspective as a goal in the fall (they may have assumed a strong academic program) talk about quality of students as a disappointment. For highlights, however, one lists the International Dinner and the other the development of an individual student. Out of sixteen teachers dealing with pre-IB or IB students, nine talk about quality of students as a disappointment. Five specifically mention low scores on IB exams. And yet a teacher who admits to feeling exam pressure and being discouraged by comments on exams from external examiners seems to see fulfillment of her intellectual and international goals; student writing has improved and the International Dinner was an exciting event. Even teachers distressed by quality of students see as highlights the blossoming of students and the fact that five of the top students in the school are IB students. Interaction of students and mixing of races are highlights for two teachers who put college preparation first as a goal. There is, however, at least some congruence between most teachers' goals and their highlights and disappointments. A social studies teacher who sees a global outlook and challenging academics as the important goals for the ISA is pleased with the International Dinner and the ninth graders. A math teacher who wants the ISA to provide the best foundation academically is also pleased with the ninth grade class. An ESL teacher who wanted students to get assimilated into our society has seen her students make a lot of progress.

As for students, their stated goals and highlights and disappointments also generally match. For example, the freshman who had identified learning about other cultures as a goal can scarcely contain her enthusiasm for that part of her experience. "I love it," she says. "A number of the families have adopted me as a sister. I'm learning some Cambodian. It's the best thing that could have happened. When you associate with foreign students you learn a lot." A better education had been her other goal, and she now looks forward to the challenge of the IB diploma. For the sophomore who thinks the ISA offers a more international point of view, that goal was met, especially through the Human Condition class. For one senior, the highlight is the completion of his studies, including the essay which he enjoyed writing and the exams. He talks about an international view gained—"I talked to a Cambodian about Pol Pot the other day"—but he wishes for more opportunity to learn about his own African roots. The other students, who saw a better education as the major goal, list as highlights "accomplishing the Psychology exam," "studying foreign policy, including writing a research paper on the dropping of the atomic bomb," "graduating in the top 10% of the class," and "seeing Washington advance in academics." The student who had gone to school in France previously is excited about the "incredible teacher/student relationships," but wishes for more international political awareness, and a senior IB student talks about events involving individuals as both highlights and disappointments, social rather than academic concerns.

In summary, the issue of identity of the International Studies Academy arises in a discussion of goals, highlights, and disappointments as it does in a discussion of the ISA as a part of Washington. For most faculty, the twin goals are an excellent education and an international perspective, but there are faculty who see academic achievement as the only or first goal, and at least at the end of the year are concerned about quality of students. One cannot generalize about the ISA student body from interviews with nine students; still, five of the nine students did not mention an international perspective in their goals, highlights, or disappointments.

Some questions may be posed. Is the ISA mainly a college preparatory program which should take only good students who will become better students? Should an excellent college preparatory program assume a global perspective? Could the two goals be made one, as they seem to be in the slogan "World leadership begins in the classroom"?

LIFE IN THE CLASSROOM

If world leadership begins in the classroom, then it is important to look at the classrooms of the International Studies Academy. What kind of teaching is going on? What are students learning? Based on observation over one school year and on student and teacher comments, three characteristics emerge. The classrooms are warm, supportive places in which intelligent, caring teachers teach students who want to learn most of the time. The teaching is mostly traditional and structured, with questioning being a major teaching technique. The curriculum is somewhat internationalized.

Visit an English as a Second Language class, for example. The topic is the environment. The teacher asks: "How do we get pollution in the air?

Does anyone not understand smoke? How do we get pollution in the water?" After each answer there is positive reinforcement: "Good" or "Beautiful." The teacher tries to involve everyone. "Jenny, you've been very quiet." "I'm going to ask someone new." "Nikita, you can't answer all the questions. You are only 1/18th of the class." They review the concept of a food chain and a student tries the example, "The tiger eats people. The people eat tiger." Everyone laughs and another student offers a more appropriate example. A student mixes up "multiply" and "butterfly," and everyone laughs good-naturedly again. The teacher defines steam, evaporation, vapor, condensation, rain, and snow. She explains to those who have come to the United States just that summer that it will be as cold as in a refrigerator by winter. This ESL class is composed of ten Cambodians, plus several Ethiopians, Jamaicans, Vietnamese, and a girl from China. The afternoon class includes the same nationalities minus Chinese, plus students from Afghanistan, Greece, and Iran.

The teacher says she loves her students and loves to teach. It is obvious. "Beautiful 's'," she says to a student who pronounces "s" properly. "Now what do we add to 'miss'? I have students who miss the motherland, miss their food. I have just thought about a student who misses a class. Go to all your classes even if you don't like them," she preaches. She knows her students well—which one came to the States from Ethiopia, who has been in a fight on the soccer team, who was probably in the army in Vietnam, which Cambodian girl is contemplating suicide. She admits she is empathetic because she remembers how it took her a half hour to read an announcement in Hebrew when she first went to Israel to teach for several years, and she remembers how it feels to be homesick. She grew up as a minority person in Detroit and taught English to Russian adult immigrants before coming to ISA in 1981. (In 1992 she is still teaching there.)

She prefers direct presentation and questioning, but there is variety in the two- and three-period-long classes. Students write book reports, do a play about Thomas Edison, practice the "We Are the World" song for an ESL progam, have a spelling bee with the winner getting a pumpkin. Mostly, however, there are questions. "How do we know she was trusting?" "What is a synonym for wreck?" "What do you do for recreation?" "What is the difference between clever and intelligent?" Always there is a smile, and a sense of humor is often evident.

The teacher of ninth grade pre-IB Ancient and Medieval World History is a midwestern native, born, bred, and schooled. Since teaching his first two years as a Peace Corps volunteer in Malaysia from 1969-71 (he had never eaten rice before he went), he has taught at Washington. His children are enrolled in the Spanish bilingual program, and his wife is completing her elementary certification. In 1981 he took his wife to

Malaysia. In 1985 he was awarded a summer Fulbright to China. (In 1992 he is still teaching in the ISA.)

Although involved in the original planning committee for the ISA back in 1977, he has been a teacher in the program for only three years. He likes the multicultural, international aspect of ISA more than the academic rigor. Athough he has strong feelings about the need for a separate wing for ISA, quality control of students, and small class size, he would also like to see cultural sensitivity sessions for the staff. For example, he told a black American student it was not appropriate for him to caress a Vietnamese girl's hair. One of the International Club advisors, he reminds others that the refugees are not foreigners but foreign-born.

In his classroom, a serious sharing of the whole world's history goes on. In October he is focusing on ancient "water cultures" and on skills. His outline is on the blackboard, and as the lesson progresses, he checks to be sure students understand meaning and spelling of words and makes suggestions for note-taking. "By the end of the year you should be able to outline on your own."

In November there are directions on the blackboard for the folder for the new grading period. The folder includes a table of contents, class and school rules, a seven-page guide on library research, a word search, a course curriculum, and an international calendar. There are assignments on the board about China and Africa, but the day's topic is Persia. Pulling down a large map of the Middle East, he talks about Persia from 1700 B.C. to 400 A.D.—government (What is a dynasty? What is a divine right monarchy?); economics (an explanation of the highway system and sea routes); religion (What is Zoroastrianism?); aggressive nationalism (What does nationalism mean?); and "peace" and prosperity for 200 years (Why is peace an ironic term?).

In December he is discussing the Greeks, in January the Romans. The students are appalled that the Spartans left weak babies to die. "It sounds very cruel," he says, "but's let's try to understand their reasons." He puts the birth of Christianity in the context of the Roman Empire. In March he is reviewing Buddhism, explaining how to pronouce some Japanese terms, and describing China's sea expeditions west. In May, Swahili proverbs appear on the blackboard.

He points out that he has internationalized the course with supplementary materials on Asia and Africa. Seeing the terms ancient and medieval as ethnocentric, he usually organizes in 200-year chunks. Finally, he says, "I constantly tell the kids that things are not gross but different."

The teacher of U.S. History and Government for tenth graders has the impossible tasks of teaching U.S. government for nine weeks and then all of U.S. history. She does it, and includes current events, too. She loves having students from foreign countries in class, and some American students say she favors Asians. Several Vietnamese students live with her, and she went to Korea on a Fulbright in summer 1984. Her room has Seoul posters on the walls and later in the year posters from the International Club Dinner of which she was a chief organizer. She likes the intellectual challenge of outstanding students, but she has energy for an eighth period regular international program class as well as for the IB classes which precede it. Students named her one of the two hardest teachers in the school, and a French student said she was the most European-like in her teaching. She has been at Washington since 1980. (In 1992 she has another job outside the classroom in the school system.)

Her eighth period International Program class begins the year with more than 30 students (in contrast to the pre-IB ninth grade class of 22), but later in the year there are usually seven or eight empty chairs. The class includes several foreign-born students and also several American students who appear to be at least potential troublemakers. But the teacher is almost unfailingly complimentary and cool. "Mr. Darnell is doing such good work" and "Thank you, James" and "You are impressing me. You are really reading." She does not get rattled by a student who hits his head (she sends him off with another student to find ice) or by a student who sticks his head in the door in the middle of class (she tells him to come back at 2:30) or by an impending snowstorm (she ignores it). She just continues to teach, emphasizing concepts and asking probing questions.

The concepts range from nationalism to containment, from confederacy to urbanization. The questions include lower-level ones like "What governments are totalitarian?" and "Who gave the Cross of Gold speech?" but also thought-provoking questions like "Can you think of examples when Adam Smith was not right?" and "Who are examples of people who wanted change badly enough to break the law?" Students occasionally ask questions, too. A foreign-born student asks, for example, about the United States not sending wheat to the Soviet Union after the Afghanistan invasion.

Her direct teaching through questioning uses study guides which she develops and sometimes textbook questions as a basis. Regular current events assignments and occasional special assignments such as writing the Preamble to the Constitution in one's own words and interviewing two foreign-born persons are also part of her curriculum. She emphasizes foreign policy, comparative political and economic systems, and geography. She wrote a World Geography curriculum one summer and would like to develop a unit on Korea for that course.

The teacher of senior IB history came to the midwest in 1968 from Long Island via college in Kentucky and after jobs in the fishing industry and rebuilding Ford and Honda engines in Puerto Rico. He went to a meeting in Milwaukee to learn about the IB program originally and started IB at Washington. He is also on the Alternative Schools Committee for the school system. For him, the challenge of working with bright students has been the bonus of ISA. (In 1992 he is the IB coordinator.)

A Chinese proverb is tacked to his lecturn in Room 538: "Man who says 'It cannot be done' should not interrupt man who is doing it." He pushes the select group of students who will take the IB exams to become thinkers and writers. He, too, refers to current events and is open to student questions. He brought up the issue of prayer at the school Thanksgiving assembly and welcomed a student's report on a Nightline segment on China. He encourages students to think about issues in history, too, as well as to learn the facts. Excerpts from a discussion on the pros and cons of imperialism are illustrative.

> Teacher: You're coming up with more good than bad on imperialism. Let's focus on the negative for a moment.
>
> Student A: People were killed. There were rebellions.
>
> Teacher: Filipinos wondered why the U.S. was doing this when it had had its own revolution?
>
> Student B: If we're imperialists, we're contradicting ourselves, our freedom and democracy. Our intentions are to help, but we aren't wanted— in Vietnam, in Lebanon.
>
> Student C: If we don't help, the Russians will.
>
> Student D: (holds up copy of Walter Rodney's *How Europe Underdeveloped Africa*.)
>
> Teacher: Who had a right to Africa?
>
> Student E: Would African civilizations have been superior if they had been left alone?

The other emphasis in the senior IB class is on the process of writing. There are individual conferences on the essay exams. In class there are reminders: "Ladies and Gentlemen. Some of you used authoritative sources the wrong way. The first sentence should state a controlling idea. The facts are coming through pretty well, but three students wrote opinion as conclusion." Later there is a concern that topics for papers be narrowed. Debate is also valued, and students are asked to interpret primary sources.

As one teacher remarked, "There are an awful lot of good people working very hard at this school." Another teacher listed "strong, progressive staff" as a major plus for the program. The four teachers just described in some detail are examples of one of the ISA's chief strengths—its faculty. There are others who are equally intelligent and caring, professional and persistent. Students recognize the quality of staff, too. When asked what they liked about the ISA, ESL students often mention friendly teachers and IP and IB students say "outstanding staff," "teachers work with student as an individual," "teachers put forth more time," "teachers care about you and push you," and "teachers know more." Although quality of students is an issue in the ISA, faculty nevertheless generally reciprocate the students' good feelings about them. "Highlight of the school year? A good group of average, intelligent kids," says one teacher. A math teacher raves about the dedication of the ESL students: "They do 99 problems instead of 10."

Students also appreciate the opportunities to analyze ideas, to find out how others feel about issues. They know if you want to talk about an idea you have to be "able to back it up." "The classes are challenging and teach you how to think," says one senior. A sophomore wishes there was an opportunity to move ahead at one's own pace. A senior wishes for more freedom—"Why English for two periods? They treat us like kindergartners." But the same senior volunteers a long paragraph of praise for what he has learned at another point in the school year. Challenging and being challenged seem to suit both faculty and students well.

As for the internationalization of the curriculum, at least three factors are at work. For the IB curriculum internationalization is built-in to some extent. Teachers also plan occasional specific activities. Finally, the curriculum is sometimes internationalized rather serendipitously by faculty and students with international experience.

The IB Contemporary History exam for May 1985 included questions on the United States, Canada, and Latin America, although since only three questions were required, a student could have done well with only a U.S. history background. There was only one question which forced students to deal with more than one area of the world. The general IB guide is heavily influenced by European education, although the range of language options is worldwide, from Swedish to Hindi to Japanese. Americans have not been successful in changing the "Study of Man" title for the curriculum section which includes philosophy (all-western syllabus), history, the social sciences, and business studies. An African-American IB student points out that he knows about Galileo and Michelangelo but little about black historical figures. Economics does list international trade and less-developed countries as topics, and Contemporary History suggests a detailed study of one area of the world, but with special emphasis on understanding the role of European power.

Besides foreign languages, which are inherently international and social studies, which can easily become international, world literature is the field which has the most potential for internationalization, and the ISA English teachers are serious in their implementation. "We're committed to world literature," says the department chair. She wants to see attitudes become less ethnocentric and wants students to realize that, living in an industrialized and rich nation, they are a minority. The classes look at not just Greek but world mythology. Chinua Achebe's *Things Fall Apart* represents African literature, and after reading *Cry the Beloved Country*, students follow the news in South Africa. After reading the *Autobiography of Malcolm X*, there is a discussion of Islam. For the teachers, this internationalization has been an education. "If it weren't for IB, I would never have read *Things Fall Apart*," says one teacher. Another, who has taught at Washington since 1965 and done *Hamlet* 54 times, has found it interesting to get into Goethe and Molière. The previous year she took students to see *Julius Caesar* done in a Nicaraguan setting.

Some specific activities which teachers build into their curricula have already been mentioned, for instance, the interviewing of foreign-born persons. A social studies teacher who teaches International Program classes in U.S. history and government, comparative government and economics, and world geography has utilized guests such as the Spanish teacher from Peru and has encouraged Southeast Asian students in her classes to make presentations on their nations. A math teacher who has students do a career education project is encouraging to students who show interest in being an interpreter or getting into international business or journalism. The teacher of physical science and chemistry notes that not all scientific discoveries were made by Americans and that acid rain is a global problem. The IB coordinator, who teaches courses entitled Technology and Culture and Theory of Knowledge, asks students to decide which world problems technology can solve and which it cannot and to learn about Muslim contributions to mathematics.

What may be as influential as the internationalized curricula, though harder to document, are the interactions that occur in class, particularly because of the foreign-born students and several bicultural teachers. In fact, sometimes American-born students get into the act, as when one student said to a fellow student from France: "I'm not American. I'm African, Jewish, and German!" A freshman tells about learning from Cambodian girls in health class, a sophomore says he learned more about Australia than algebra from an Australian boy in his class, and a junior speaks of a classmate from Sri Lanka.

The teacher who lived in Kenya for 10 years said she thought students had learned more cross-cultural information than biology from her in her first year in the ISA. In October during one class period she mentioned a television program that night on Nairobi, explained why salad greens would have to be washed in Clorox in Kenya, and used an example of a Kenyan researcher doing an experiment similar to the one they were doing to test for oil in seeds. Students ask her questions about Kenya, but they're not interested in visiting there, she says.

The biology teacher is not the only bicultural faculty member. The French teacher came originally as an AFS high school exchange student, returned for college, and stayed. "I try to instill internationalism," he says. "At least they can say they knew a Frenchman and they can come back and ask whether that Frenchman who used to teach us about how they drive and eat is still there." Spanish students can say they knew a Peruvian. In her first full year in ISA, the Spanish teacher from Peru has been very involved in activities such as the Spanish Club and the International Club. In her classes the students talk about topics like male and female roles in Latin America and racism. She has tried to find Spanish-speaking pen pals and she opens her classroom during lunch for students who want to talk in Spanish.

Other faculty are not bicultural, but are internationally experienced through travel. The IB coordinator, whose grandparents came from Germany, has traveled to western and eastern Europe and Latin America. In 1984 a teacher had a Fulbright to Korea, the counselor went to China, and the Ford Foundation grant director at the school went to Japan. In the summer of 1985, Fulbrights were awarded to two social studies teachers, one for India and one for China. The German teacher attended the Goethe Institute in Germany. The associate principal went to Peru for a month. Another social studies teacher traveled to Europe for the first time, and a science teacher visited relatives in France.

The impact of these internationally experienced persons is not easy to measure. The French teacher is afraid many students would expect to take the interstate highway south to get to France. The Ford grant director's trip to Japan showed the most school spin-off, including pen pal projects and a videotape prepared jointly with the Korea Fulbrighter. Both spoke to faculty for after school meetings, and six classes saw slides of Japan.

Sharing experiences is more difficult for students. A sophomore who was born in Paris, has a French mother and an Indian father, and has been around the world twice finds teachers and students friendly. However, back several weeks from a month-long vacation during which she went to China and India and then France, she had not shared that experience with teachers or students and did not expect to. She speaks English well, but ESL students do not, so their communication is even more limited. Still, an Ethiopian student talked with American-born students about the famine, and a Cambodian student wrote a report on Cambodia for geography class. The student from Afghanistan reported at the end of the year that he had conversed with students but not teachers about his country. The student from Greece had never been asked to share her knowledge with a world history class.

The ESL teachers have made a special effort to connect foreign-born students and American-born students outside ISA. In one class American-born occupational students who are considered potential dropouts and troublemakers helped ESL students each week with language work-sheets. The students also had a social gathering at Halloween when they made masks and taught each other games. In another class, home economics, nursing, and cosmetology students helped ESL students learn to thread sewing machines, read thermometers, and understand American hairstyles.

There is no doubt that much teaching and learning are occurring in the International Studies Academy. Probably because, as an alternative school, the ISA can choose its teachers, the faculty are special people. Many students are, too. Probably because an internationalized curricu-lum does not rank as an equal with the first two characteristics of class-room life in the ISA, identity rises as an issue yet again. World leader-ship can begin in the classroom. That is beginning to happen in the ISA, but international perspective is not a fully integrated ingredient of the curriculum yet. Of course, classrooms are not the only places in which students and teachers in the ISA have opportunities to become inter-national. Special events also play a role.

SPECIAL EVENTS

In the United States, schools are more than the sum of life in class-rooms. Extracurricular activities and special events also contribute to the school experience. ISA students participate in many extracurricular activities at Washington, from the band to the International Club. The latter is particularly important in extending the ISA slogan that world leadership begins in the classroom. The club's dinner and program in March was a major special event; it was listed as a highlight of the year by the associate principal and several teachers who were club sponsors and was also mentioned by several students. Other special events which took advantage of the international perspective of the ISA were the visit in February by a group of international ISA students to the Bilingual Academy middle school and the foreign language classes' poetry read-ing in May.

The International Dinner recognized the sentiment announced in a poster in several ISA classrooms: "America is Many, Count Me In." The program included presentations by the language clubs, dances from Cambodia and Vietnam, Martin Luther King's "I Have a Dream" speech, some Jamaican reggae music, and an American square dance. The most enthusiastic reception was given to a lively Cambodian coconut dance with three boys dressed in yellow shirts and red sashes and three girls wearing pink. The finale square dance was presented by black and white American-born students and the student from Afghanistan who fol-lowed his partner carefully as she swung him around. Measured by numbers in attendance, the dinner was a huge success. About 300 people came instead of the expected 150. The central administration of the school district was well represented, including the superintendent, but the crowd was mostly students, parents, and teachers.

In terms of student participation before as well as during, the event was also a success. Club members had a fine time preparing for the dinner, making a big "We are the World" sign and setting the tables with flowers from the school greenhouse. The ESL students made map and flag posters to represent their countries.

But the parents may have gained the most. As the dinner began, one mother of a white American student remarked how different high school was now. She asked her daughter about the status of the international students, whether they were here permanently or temporarily. Her daughter didn't know and didn't seem concerned. She introduced her mother to a friend from Sri Lanka and admiringly pointed out another classmate whose first language is French, who now speaks excellent English, and who that night was singing with the Spanish Club. Then the daughter went off with the black class president to help serve Kool-Aid to the overflowing crowd.

The mother would have found it instructive to have heard the Afghan student, the Sri Lankan student, and the French/Indian student sharing their experiences with middle school students at the Bilingual Academy. The high school students told the younger pupils about the International Studies Academy and about their own backgrounds in a special assembly in February. Standing before more than a hundred students, the Afghan teenager told about walking for a week to get out of Afghanistan and studying English for a month and a half in a camp in Pakistan before coming to the United States. "Now I have learned to talk," he said, "and I have friends. I am happy to have the opportunity to go to college in the future and learn electrical engineering."

Next the Sri Lankan student explained that her family had come to the United States for better opportunities, especially in education. She was very positive about her experience at Washington. "Americans make us feel accepted. Even the principal makes me feel accepted." The middle school students were fascinated by her description of her all-girls school in Sri Lanka where uniforms were required. "I haven't decided whether to go back to Sri Lanka," she said. "It will be the toughest decision of my life."

The student who is the daughter of a French mother and an Indian father compared French and American schools and then described her Christmas trip to China and India. "I found it very interesting to communicate with people in China in spite of the language barrier," she said. "It was similar in India, although I had the advantage of visiting my family. These experiences made me start to learn not to judge people by their appearance but more from the inside. I think it is good to realize that there are so many different people with different cultures and languages on this earth."

Later in the spring at the poetry reading this international student read a poem in Spanish entitled "Pienso." Translated, it reads:

Life is a struggle.
A struggle about, towards liberty
A struggle about knowing oneself
A struggle for love.
To try to love
Love humanity
A humanity in big need of love
Because love is the only remedy
In a world of hate
It's the only thing we have left.

The poetry reading was in honor of the director of the school system's bilingual program, ESL program, and foreign languages who was taking another job in Washington, D.C. and who had known some of the students since they entered the bilingual program as kindergartners. A warm, comfortable affair with hugging, tears, carnations, and roses, it involved the students who had contributed to the booklet of poems, some parents and teachers and guests, including an AFS Chinese exchange teacher from another school and visiting journalists from the Netherlands and Spain.

Paint may have been peeling on the low wall behind the lectern where the students stood to read their poetry in Spanish, French, and German, some hesitantly, some fluently, but an international community was present and a sense of community was obvious. During the punch and cookies, several students talked with the visiting European journalists about American politics and the Indian father recently back from China spoke with the Chinese exchange teacher.

A feeling of community was one important outcome of the special events like the dinner and the poetry reading. Another was recognition of students' talents, obvious in the middle school program as well as at the dinner and poetry reading. Both outcomes, which are also rationales for such activities, apply to other special events like the Brotherhood Assembly which involved the whole school and the International Baccalaureate reception which involved only the IB students and their parents. A feeling of community is also relevant to the issue of ISA identity. None of the special events described involved all the ISA students, but they did utilize the expertise of some students in things international—dance, cross-cultural experience, foreign language learn-ing—to build a program of sharing with each other and with others beyond the ISA.

Although such events create a sense of community and show students as experts, they mask as well as elevate the everyday reality. Although one American-born freshman may have spoken for others when she said that everyone enjoyed the International Dinner and would now pursue an international perspective more vigorously, another student, a sophomore, is probably more realistic. He found it interesting to hear the Dutch journalist's description of western European nations as U.S. satellites, and he worked hard preparing for the dinner, making neatly-lettered signs for the entrance. Yet at the end of the school year he reflected:

> From the outside you see blacks, whites, foreign students in classes, and it looks good, but it's not really a community. It can't happen in one day like the International Dinner. It has to be continual process, making one friend at a time, maybe in class, maybe on the soccer team. Students do help each other with homework and there's more community at higher grade levels. But I don't see the Southeast Asians being integrated. They're isolated too much. Until American and foreign students are forced to work together, the community will not be there.

Community, then, is in the "becoming" stage. And the question arises: What kind of community? Especially for immigrants, the ques-tion relates to assimilation, joining or being pulled into the square dance. As the Afghan student's ESL teacher asked, "How long are you the foreign student? How long do the Vietnamese perform their dances?" The freshman girl already sees an answer in her Cambodian friends who are wearing American clothes to school, riding 10-speed bikes, and even occasionally marrying Americans. The teacher who lived in Kenya for 10 years says: "I don't think foreign students are bringing in their treasures as much as they are being assimilated." Does the ISA want to be the kind of community in which various world cul-tures are recognized and shared? If so, how can immigrants and others with international experience share their "treasures," make their coun-tries remembered, and broaden the vision of community? The struggle between melting pot and salad bowl continues, and there are no easy answers.

THE FUTURE

As the International Studies Academy grows and develops and changes, two key issues loom large. They are not problems to be solved, but rather questions to be continually considered. Both are identity issues in the sense that they relate to how the administrators, teachers, and students of the ISA perceive themselves and perceive the Academy. Both are issues recognized and in fact raised by those involved with the ISA. They may be stated as follows: How can the ISA help students achieve academic excellence and gain a global perspective? How can the ISA become an international educational community which encourages students and teachers to become world citizens?

The first question takes for granted that the International Studies Academy sees both academic excellence and a global perspective as important. The second focuses on the ideal of community which the two administrators expound as a goal and which various students and teachers refer to, whether to wish for more physical togetherness in the building or to describe the senior IB class as "family." From that community students and teachers go out into the world community as individual citizens.

Academic excellence and a global perspective are compatible, of course. In fact, it is hard to imagine a person being described as truly educated who is not cognizant of the world so that he or she can contribute to that world. Still, there are those whose vision of the educated person focuses more on knowledge of western heritage than on cross-cultural awreness.

Although extensive foreign language opportunities and requirements, the IB curriculum, teacher-planned activities, and the internationalization due to internationally experienced teachers and students contribute to the infusion of a global perspective, no one feels the curriculum has been internationalized enough. Few students are affected systematically. Students who have not attended the bilingual program may not start a foreign language until they come to Washington. The International Baccalaureate curriculum is more international in clientele (it is in schools worldwide) than in curriculum (it is heavily influenced by a European model of education). The Program students are generally thought to be getting a less internationalized curriculum than IB students. ESL students are often placed in regular comprehensive classes, although the associate principal would like ISA teachers to take on the ESL students. Teacher-planned activities which emphasize a global perspective are fairly few and scattered, a Spaceship Earth exercise here, *The Good Earth* there. The impact of internationally experienced persons depends on whether a student has such a teacher or is in class with such a student.

Clearly the IB program has been carefully developed and is the centerpiece of the Academy. Teachers get very direct aid from yearly IB conferences and from IB materials and have a specific goal—the IB exam—which they work toward in concert with the students. There are those teachers who wonder if the effort is worth it, especially immediately after the exams. Several teachers are cynical about the IB's durability, given the very small number of diploma candidates and the cost. (But in 1992 more ISA students are taking exams and the school district is still paying the increased cost. Other IB changes: the number of schools worldwide using IB has grown; the 11th and 12th grade curriculum is more rigid; IB is computerized; the outside examiner system is gone.) Quality of students has already been raised as an issue teachers talked about, especially when the worth of the IB is measured by exam performance. The exam, however, is only a measure of academic achievement, not a measure of attainment of a global perspective. One way to put a global perspective on a par with academic excellence as a goal and outcome might be to test it with a decision-making situation, either as a final essay or as a small group project.

"Becoming international" was as far as a generalization about the ISA was going to go. However, in interviews and more informal conversations another word kept coming up—community. The IB coordinator talks about a community of scholars being the hope of the world, for instance. Teachers and students tend to see community a bit less esoterically, but nonetheless as important. The following ideas and dreams, all from teachers, relate to international community building in very practical ways. Some are related to building a physical community, a place or places clearly identified as ISA. Others are programmatic, urging that the ISA be brought together for more special events and that there be more opportunities for international connections with the world community. Parenthetical statements explain their status in 1992.

1. Make the ISA a separate wing. (This proposal was drawn up by several teachers and presented to the school adminstration in May 1985. Shortly after the end of school, a decision was made to put departments in contiguous classrooms, a halfway measure. Not all teachers were in favor of a separate wing, and the rationale for keeping ISA integrated within the school has continued to be stronger.)

2. Make floors/departments continents and individual classrooms countries. Put posters from different countries in the halls. (This was not implemented, but the associate principal, now principal, mentioned it as a possibility for the future in 1992.)

3. Hold ISA assemblies, including a songfest, a Christmas program, an assembly in which ISA students learned about immigrant students' journeys to the United States. (This has happened.)

4. Hold full-day seminars on special topics or more frequent half-day seminars. (A variant has happened—see #8.)

5. Extend exchange of teachers within the school—French teacher would be willing to speak on the French Revolution and on French-speaking

West Africa; Peruvian teacher has already visited some classes; teachers who have traveled should be utilized as guest lecturers. (This has not happened.)

6. Have foreign language week in which German classes teach German to Spanish and French students and vice versa. (This has not happened.)

7. Organize big brother/big sister program for new foreign-born students. (This was organized for the whole Academy.)

8. Continue encouragement of more people from different cultural backgrounds as visitors—foreign dignitaries, dancers, poets, politicians. (The Council on World Affairs has adopted the International Studies Academy. Speakers sponsored by the Council usually come to ISA as well for an assembly or a faculty meeting and one teacher and five students go to each Council meeting. For example, a member of the National Security Council spoke at a faculty meeting in 1992.)

9. Increase international exchange—expansion of numbers of exchange students going to and coming from Latin America and Europe, encouragement for attendance at international conferences by teachers. (By 1992, three exchange programs were in place in which teachers and students exchanged three weeks/three weeks with teachers and students in three places—Paris, France; Freiburg, Germany; and Vigo, Spain. About 35 students participated each year, and the school district paid for the teachers' substitutes.)

10. Get financial support for mock United Nations team to go to New York, perhaps from local business. (This has not happened.)

11. Organize an International Day for the whole school in which everyone comes in costume. (This has not happened.)

The ultimate goal of the ISA community, of course, is for the individual to leave the IB "family" or the ISA friends and emerge as a world citizen. Teachers take that step, too, when they travel or leave temporarily for another position. The IB English teacher was in Japan for the 1985-86 school year, and a social studies teacher worked in a district evaluation team for the two years following the school year described here. Perhaps most interesting was that the ISA secretary for two years, whose rapport with and savvy about students were special, left to find a job in the travel industry. Internationalness was thrust upon her, and she responded.

The students, even the younger ones, seem to know who they are. Besides student, the roles of their lives have included model, football player, school announcer, band member, friend, and will include pediatrician, nurse, perhaps missionary, probably parents. They will also be world citizens. Answers to the question "What would you do about the famine in Africa?" showed that some ISA students are beginning to think as world citizens. The students show some understanding of distribution, political, and ecological factors. They suggest long-term, multilateral aid. They are concerned about the hungry in this country as well. One would adopt a child in response. Another says the nuclear arms buildup must be stopped so money can be spent on other things.

Several seniors said in May 1985 that they felt like pioneers. Students, teachers, and administrators were all pioneers in this magnet school becoming international—figuring out its identity, trying to meld academic excellence and a global perspective, working on building community.

In 1985 the associate principal, one of the pioneers, quoted the Chilean poet Pablo Neruda that we are "residents of the earth." She spoke of education as a "living, growing thing." She often talked about a "community of learners," and one of her goals for herself was to be bilingual in English and Spanish. In talking about her vision, she set a standard for an international educational community at the International Studies Academy at Washington High School. In September 1992, as new principal for Washington High School, she continued to be visionary. She talked about other achievements of the last seven years, beyond changes already mentioned: an International Studies Seminar which was a welcoming experience for all ISA students, teaching them goals and objectives of ISA and concepts of global and multicultural education; a year-long course on the arts from an international perspective; the requiring of the Human Condition course for all; the integration of ESL students into ISA, especially IB courses. But she also talked about the future. She wants all Washington students to be required to take four years of math, science, English, and social studies. The school is making an aggressive effort to help all students pass the proficiency tests mandated by the state, and she sees the International Baccalaureate common educational exam as a good model to expand upon. She wants the whole school to be an international school, and all the courses to be globalized. "Students need this for the 21st century. All students can benefit."

Academic excellence *and* a global perspective, an educational community preparing students to become world citizens—those goals for the International Studies Academy now may become goals for all of Washington High School.

Chapter 9

Utilizing International Experience: Ideas for Implementation

> When we come together, we form our own nation
> of travelers, of in-betweens. Even where we've blended,
> stopped trying to explain, we meet our own again and
> know each other—this one understands, we speak the same
> memories, dream ourselves in the same overloaded truck
> rattling and bumping along in a cloud of dust as we sing.
>
> (Rambo, 1992)

> I was still young when I recognized that giving money to all the
> lepers on the streets of Dakar would not redress the world's social
> injustices.
>
> (Schaetti, 1992)

The poem "Travelers," from which the first quotation is taken, was written for a school reunion of "global nomads," persons who lived overseas as children because their parents were working overseas, in this case in Zaire. For schools, the challenge is to encourage internationally experienced persons of all kinds—the global nomad, the returned Peace Corps volunteer, the exchange student, the exchange student returnee, the refugee or immigrant—to share some of those memories with those who have not traveled. Remember returned Peace Corps volunteer Karl who told his story of riding on top of an orange truck in Morocco to his young students. But sharing knowledge only represents half the possibilities. Internationally experienced persons also have perceptual understanding to share, an awareness that Schaetti explains following the example from her childhood living in Dakar—the second quotation. She writes: "Complex challenges require comprehensive solutions, a multiplicity of approaches and the weaving of many strands into a web supporting the movements of change" (1992, 4). Schaetti is referring to the complex challenge of injustice, but global education is also a complex challenge— especially the role of internationally experienced persons in global education.

What are some comprehensive solutions to the utilization of internationally experienced persons? What are some examples of multiple approaches? How can the solutions and the approaches be woven together to support a movement of change—education with a global perspective in K–12 schools?

COMPREHENSIVE SOLUTIONS

Comprehensive solutions demand attention to the big picture in at least three ways. First, the utilization of internationally experienced persons takes place in schools, and although individual internationally experienced teachers can and do enhance their own classroom teaching —can and do make an impact on their own students (consider chapters 3, 4, and 5)—the whole school should be the focus of comprehensive solutions which involve internationally experienced teachers and students. Second, the contribution of internationally experienced persons needs to be set in the framework of a combined multicultural/global perspective which recognizes the overlap in concerns of diverse groups, such as Bennett (1990) has developed, or in the context of diversity, as Cushner (1992) advocates. Third, schools are located in communities which may be home to other internationally experienced persons, so schools should make connections with other institutions such as colleges, universities, and museums.

The Individual School and Change

Tye and Tye (1992) make a persuasive case for seeing the individual school as site for change, with other school district and state personnel acting in supportive, facilitating ways, and an outside agency (perhaps a university) providing a linkage to the new knowledge needed. Their research on their own catalytic work in reaching out from the Center for Human Interdependence (CHI) at Chapman College to foster global education within 11 schools in Orange County, California is particularly important because of what they learned about how change can happen and why it may not. They explain the deep structure of school culture, the pressures on teachers, the role of principals.

In terms of global education, the Tyes also accept that the optimum time to work on change is probably when society is in a transition period; thus global education's time is now because our society is becoming globalized. Their definition of global education (below), which evolved over time and was purposely not developed until the third year of the project, relates nicely to the substantive knowledge and perceptual understanding aspects of the impact of international experience model presented in chapter 2.

> Global education involves 1) the study of problems and issues which cut across national boundaries, and the interconnectedness of cultural, environmental, economic, political, and technological systems, and 2) the cultivation of cross-cultural understanding, which includes development of the skill of "perspective taking"—that is, being able to see life from someone else's point of view. Global perspectives are important at every grade level, in every curricular subject area, and for all children and adults. (Tye and Tye, 1992, 87)

Over four years, several types of programs were developed in the CHI network of schools: infusion programs, special projects initiated by the network teachers, and special projects initiated by CHI through small grants. CHI provided the linkage to information about global education through a library and two full-time staff members who were facilitating interventionists, delivering resources and services, spending most of their time helping teachers in their schools. Following are only a few examples of global education in the CHI schools. Infusion programs developed by teachers included a two-month interdisciplinary unit for second-third grade students on how clothing connects them to other places and people in the world; a collaboration between a high school English and high school home economics teachers using short stories from around the world and food and fashion from those same countries; and a foreign language telecommunications project with sister schools in Japan, Colombia, and France. Special teacher-initiated projects included an annual evening experience of a region's or nation's culture for parents presented by a seventh grade team and their students and often drawing on teachers' international experiences; a survey about racism at a high school; and a Walk in the Real World for upper middle class suburban white seventh graders through ethnic neighborhoods in downtown Los Angeles. One CHI-initiated project was an Orange County in the World project modeled on the Columbus in the World project, originally developed at Ohio State University and now widely copied. CHI also provided mini-grants. For example, one grant allowed disabled students to receive instructional materials and a field trip to the zoo as part of a unit on endangered species and another allowed a high school guidance department to purchase computer software which would give students information about peace and international studies programs available in U.S. colleges and universities (Tye and Tye, 1992, 95-101).

Looking at the CHI project as a model, it is clear that an individual school can successfully be the locus for making education with a global perspective a focus of curriculum activity, while taking into account the competing demands on teachers' time and the uniqueness of the single school and staff, especially the principal. One can imagine internationally experienced persons playing important roles in such curriculum change.

Multiculturalism and Internationalism

The role of internationally experienced teachers and students also needs to be set in the context of a combined multicultural/international framework. Barber describes classrooms as "workshops for overcoming prejudice" (1992, 97). Bennett and Cushner would agree. Bennett integrates Hanvey's dimensions of a global perspective with goals of multicultural education, resulting in the following list:

Goal 1. To develop multiple historical perspectives

Goal 2. To strengthen cultural consciousness

Goal 3. To strengthen intercultural competence

Goal 4. To combat racism, prejudice, and discrimination

Goal 5. To increase awareness of the state of the planet and global dynamics

Goal 6. To build social action skills

Core values in her model are "responsibility to a world community, reverence for the earth, acceptance and appreciation of cultural diversity, and respect for human dignity and universal human rights" (Bennett, 1990, 282).

Bennett's combination of the multicultural and the international forces educators to do more than dramatize folk tales and plan international dinners and more than discuss ethnic conflict in other countries or do a decision-making simulation about so-called third world nations, although the former are excellent starting places for gaining cross-cultural awareness and the latter may make discussion of such issues at home more fruitful. Teachers and students are encouraged to think globally but act locally. Combating racism is right there on the list, so it is impossible to avoid engaging in a discussion of race, beginning "not with the problems of black people, but with the flaws of American society—flaws rooted in historic inequalities and longstanding cultural stereotypes" (West, 1992). Of course, one way to become aware of one's own perspective is to study the "other," for example, to put racism in a global perspective. The study of images of Africa may be revealing for students who deal every day with stereotypes of eastern Kentucky. Seeing the movie "The Dry White Season" set in South Africa or "Mister Johnson" set in Nigeria is instructive. But racism must also be attacked by studying about *and* interacting in the United States. The study of Japan led by a teacher who has lived there and can teach students how to speak some Japanese and write haiku will be valuable, but students should also learn about the Japanese-American experience and the experience of other Asian Americans in the United States (Takaki, 1989).

In *Human Diversity in Education: An Integrative Approach*, Cushner begins with stories which speak about the complexity of "experiences people have with the fact of human diversity" (1992, 3) and concludes by advocating a curriculum transformation which strives to achieve multiple perspectives, addresses issues of diversity in all disciplines, requires active student participation, and involves the local community. In between the beginning and the end, gender and exceptionality, as well as culture, are dealt with in the context of diversity.

Placing the contribution of internationally experienced teachers and students in the larger framework of multicultural/global perspectives or in the context of human diversity allows that contribution to be in the middle, at the heart of the curriculum, rather than at the margin. The American first grader who lived in Fiji and Sierra Leone before coming "home" and the Asian Indian first grader born in the United States while his parents went to graduate school are two children with stories to tell, like the first grader with leg braces and the first grader who came from another state to live with her grandmother.

The teacher in that classroom can learn those children's stories and the stories of her other students, include them in the curriculum, and invite the parents and the grandmother to participate in the curriculum as well. Families are a first community resource. To build a global perspective, internationally experienced teachers and students at local institutions of higher education may be a second resource. If one defines community as those who communicate, community is expandable and expansive. Thus a rural school in a border state communicates with an urban school in another border state through a telecommunications linkage. A suburban American school communicates with a school in Russia through video letters.

MULTIPLE APPROACHES

Multiple approaches follow logically from an acceptance of multiple perspectives. An individual teacher, a school, or a teacher education program can utilize international experience. Possible approaches by a school, a university, and the community working separately are described below, followed by a list of ways in which they can cooperate as strands woven into a web.

Schools

1. The school mission statement should include a clearly stated goal that students will gain a global perspective as part of educational preparation for citizenship in the 21st century.

This goal should be carried out through an infusion of a global perspective and the utilization of internationally experienced persons in all subject areas—especially social studies, but also language, math, science, arts, physical education, home economics. An elementary physical education teacher might teach international games in conjunction with several international students in the school or international people in the community. A home economics teacher might do a unit on cross-cultural child development and get students involved in a Peace Corps Partnership where they collect books for an elementary school in an African nation. An example of a social studies teacher utilizing international experience is Appendix 1. A list of examples of utilization of internationally experienced students and teachers and the related area of impact of international experience from the model in chapter 2 is Appendix 2.

2. The leadership of the superintendent and administrators, such as principals and curriculum supervisors, is important.

Some use of international experience in individual classrooms can happen without such leadership, but more can be done with it. A superintendent can decide that international education is important enough to warrant part- or full-time attention by someone in the system. That person might be the liaison with the community (as in such organizations as youth exchange and Sister Cities) and college or university, if available. Depending on size of system and makeup of student body, that person might have responsibilities ranging from dealing with contributions and problems of limited English-speaking students to organizing school exchange programs, from promoting teacher opportunities such as the Fulbright programs to facilitating the development of culture kits by traveling teachers. Appendix 3 makes suggestions about how to organize for the utilization of internationally experienced persons in a school system.

3. Hiring policies should encourage internationally experienced persons to apply for all jobs and personnel policies should encourage summer and sabbatical study—travel and exchange.

Job applications should have a place to list international experience. Persons with international experience because of national origin or through exchange, study abroad, student teaching overseas, the Peace Corps, business, armed services, or private voluntary organizations, including churches, should be recruited because of that experience. This policy should connect with a strong affirmative action program. Persons who are of "minority" backgrounds, and thus have "inside the United States" cross-cultural experience, can have some of the same assets that internationally experienced persons often possess. Teachers and administrators should be encouraged to be short-term international sojourners and to participate in longer exchanges and sabbatical possibilities. Money might be raised locally for travel fellowships, and information on partially or fully funded opportunities, such as those in Japan for social studies teachers, should be disseminated. Reflecting upon and sharing the learning in some way should be required, perhaps through local and school newspaper articles and television programs, perhaps through an annual International Connection dinner and program.

4. *Ten percent of the high school student body should be involved in exchange each year.*

The 10% figure was suggested at an international education conference by an IBM executive who was born in India. It assumes students coming from other countries and American students going to other countries on a variety of exchange programs existent in schools and communities already, including both group travel and individual home-stay and lasting several weeks, a summer, or a year. It assumes some responsibility taken by the schools to work with and develop programs which are following government guidelines. Orientation and returnee workshops are important. Students should be required to keep some sort of journal or do some kind of project in connection with the experience which ideally would be planned and/or shared with at least a teacher and class; students may, in some cases, receive credit. As for teachers and administrators, formal recognition and public relations and education are appropriate. Again, money can be raised locally for travel scholarships, and eligible students should also be encouraged to apply for programs fully or partially paid for by government such as Congress/ Bundestag and Japan Senate or by corporations or service clubs. Consideration should be given to arranging exchanges which are cross-cultural within the United States and with North America (Canada and Mexico) where expenses will be more reasonable. Appendix 4 describes 20 ways exchange students and exchange returnees can contribute to schools.

5. *An International Studies magnet school or program and at least one world language which is not the traditional French, German, or Spanish should be available in each medium-sized and large system, and otherwise on a regional or state basis.*

Some students will be particularly interested in international affairs as a content area or a career goal or as the best preparation to be a citizen in the 21st century. There are many models for international school programs. One is included in this book as a case study. In some states, a statewide summer program like that in Pennsylvania may be an alternative. The more exotic world language could be tied into the international studies magnet program. As at Washington High School, students from bilingual elementary and middle school programs can go on to attend an international magnet program. The International Baccalaureate is an increasingly popular possibility, but it will rarely be the only appropriate way for students to get a more specialized international eduation. International education should not be limited to an elite group. Neither should world languages be considered only the province of college-bound high school students. Immigrant and exchange students should be considered as potential magnet program pupils, preferably integrated into the program as contributors while given help with English. Finally, magnet and language programs should not be limited to high school students. In fact, creative interdisciplinary global teaching will be easier to implement at elementary and middle schools and could happen at a magnet for the performing arts as well as at a bilingual program.

  6. *Extracurricular and co-curricular activities should involve both internationally and non-internationally experienced students in issues and in service.*

International clubs, such as the one at Washington High School, are perhaps the most common high school extracurricular activity. Language clubs are also often active. Typical activities sponsored by such organizations are international dinners and presentations by returning exchange students or visiting international students. Sometimes other clubs such as Harambee or Future Homemakers or Future Farmers will have programs and projects related to other countries. Another popular activity which brings students from many schools together is the mock United Nations Assembly, sometimes sponsored by the YMCA, sometimes by a university. In Michigan there is a mock Organization of African States. Such programs are excellent opportunities for utilizing the expertise of immigrants, exchange students, international students at colleges and universities, returned Peace Corps volunteers and other internationally experienced people. Service projects should also be encouraged through classes, clubs, and Student Councils. Heifer Project and the Peace Corps Partnership Program are two programs with which schools can work.

HIGHER EDUCATION AND TEACHER EDUCATION

  1. *A global perspective and international experience are important for faculty in both teacher education and the larger institution.*

It seems obvious that one way to internationalize the schools of the future is to internationalize the education of future teachers, as Taylor's

The World as Teacher pointed out 20 years ago. To facilitate that, hiring, grant, and sabbatical policies should support international experience for faculty. Some faculty will get their international experience through study abroad, others through exchange, research, conferences, consulting, or development projects.

2. *The curriculum for future teachers should include the requirement of academic courses which have cross-cultural content, and multicultural and international content should be included in professional courses as well.*

Academic courses which have cross-cultural content include those in such disciplines as languages, anthropology, economics, geography, history, political science, literature, and the arts. Teachers do need to be knowledgeable. Someone once said that the American problem in Vietnam was that we didn't know who the Vietnamese were. Teachers have similar problems if they don't know anything about the countries of origin of their immigrant or visiting international students.

Coursework in education should deal with multicultural concerns such as treating students as individuals *and* in the context of their cultures, as well as developing curricula which teach about the diversity of cultures and about international issues. Social studies methods courses are particularly important. A social studies methods course could be internationalized through a demonstration unit on an international issue which illustrates how materials are gathered, how concepts and skills are chosen, how activities and evaluation are developed (see Appendix 5), but other skills and topics are also critical. A survey of 30 teacher education programs which prepare secondary social studies teachers to teach with a global perspective concluded that teachers are not receiving preparation to teach U.S. and world history courses from a global perspective, or to teach students to think globally when making local decisions. Teachers are also not being prepared to teach about international organizations and multinational corporations or about environment and technology (Merryfield, 1991).

3. *Every teacher education student should demonstrate participation in cross-cultural experiences, and the option to student teach in a cultural setting different from one's own should be available.*

Besides gaining a global perspective and developing self and relationships, there are several other reasons why teacher education students should have cross-cultural experiences. One is that teaching itself is a cross-cultural encounter, as is evident in the case studies. A second is that characteristics of interculturally effective people are relevant to effective teaching (Wilson, 1982). How students might be required to include intercultural experiences in their teacher education program is illustrated in Appendix 6. Student teaching in other cultural settings, from Indian reservations to American schools overseas to schools in English-speaking countries, is possible in individual college programs and through consortia arrangements. Such programs demand careful management, serious screening and orientation, and requirements for reflection on learning. Teacher education students, especially those in social studies and languages, should also be encouraged to consider regular study abroad programs. After graduation, there are opportunities for math, science, and English as a Second Language teachers in the Peace Corps and for teachers of English in Japan, as well as possibilities in American and international schools overseas, usually after some stateside experience.

4. *Graduate course, inservice program, and study tour opportunities should be available for teachers.*

Global and comparative education courses should be offered for teachers, as well as summer school courses, institutes, and workshops on specialized topics such as The Middle East or Teaching about Africa. Sometimes teachers enjoy going to another part of the United States or to another country for an intensive institute or study tour, such as those sponsored by Fulbright or organized by universities. However, many teachers cannot participate in such programs, and colleges and universities should work with local school systems to offer shorter courses and study tours, with follow-up, which meet curriculum and personal needs of teachers.

COMMUNITY

1. *Youth exchange should be promoted by reputable organizations.*

Youth exchange programs should work closely with the schools and with each other when possible. Those programs could be the catalyst for organizing a World Issues Forum for internationally and non-internationally experienced young people or a special day in the state capital or a social event.

2. *Local international organizations should consider programming for young people and teachers.*

International organizations such as world affairs councils, United Nations Associations, Sister Cities, and service clubs should publicize their programs to schools. Social studies teachers and students should be invited to hear relevant speakers or attend internationally related exhibits or performances. Internationally experienced students and teachers may be attractive speakers for such organizations' meetings, too. Establishment of local essay contests and prizes may be appropriate. Children's museums and art museums often host exhibits which are international. In large metropolitan areas, there are many such opportunities. Communitywide events such as ethnic heritage and international festivals give the community a global perspective.

WEAVING THE STRANDS TOGETHER

Schools, universities, and communities can also work together, weaving the multiple approaches into cooperative ventures that support education for a global perspective.

Even small, isolated communities almost always include some non-school, internationally experienced people who can be resources. A Vietnam veteran may visit an American history class. A Filipino doctor may visit a sixth grade world geography class. Sometimes the outreach of a university can bring the world to such a school, as in the case of Cornwall Middle School.

In other situations, like those at Beech Valley Elementary School and Washington High School, there are many resources available among parents and in the community, but they do need to be organized. In some places, the university (a teacher education program, an area studies outreach office, a global education project, an international student office) may be the catalyst.

One example is an annual day-long international fair at a college of education, planned jointly with local teachers. Classes contribute either an exhibit or a performance. Besides seeing one another's contributions, the students visit college classrooms where activities are organized by junior high language classes, campus international student groups, and community clubs. Students from elementary social studies methods classes act as guides, stamp passports, and help with set-up and clean-up.

Museum exhibits offer another illustration of school/university/ community cooperation. A children's museum might have a regularly changing cultural exhibit put together with the help of university and community people from a particular country, and they might organize school programming to accompany the exhibit. An art museum might host a photography or textile or other exhibit from a particular culture and enhance it with local contributions and programming related to the culture, including inservice for teachers.

Appendix 7 shows examples of cooperation to support education for a global perspective.

CONCLUSION

Harlan Cleveland, who has worked in international education for more than 50 years, spoke to K–college educators at a 1991 conference about the goals of education with a global perspective. "There has to be room in our American philosophy," he said, "and in our American classrooms, for three ideas. And we have to be able, and develop in our children the capacity, to hold these three ideas in our minds at the same time." Cleveland's ideas are ones which appear in this book and are appropriate to emphasize as a conclusion: that nations, peoples, and learnings are interdependent; that group differences are valuable—in fact, that difference is an added value; and that a just society will judge people as persons, not as categories (Cleveland, 1991, 6).

Internationally experienced persons have probably learned about those ideas firsthand. Their actions as cultural mediators can help the young people of this country hold those ideas in their hands, and in their heads and hearts.

Appendixes

APPENDIX 1: UTILIZING INTERNATIONAL EXPERIENCE
IN A SOCIAL STUDIES CLASS

As he read the autobiographical statements students wrote the first day of class, Mr. Rowe, the teacher of American government, noted that Celeste was just back from a summer in Switzerland as an exchange student, Jacques was an exchange student who had recently arrived from France to spend the year as an exchange student in the United States, and Amin had come from Egypt to live with his university professor uncle and go to high school. "How," wondered Mr. Rowe, "can these three students add to my class?"

He knew there would be many opportunities for comparisons to be made in general class discussion, whether the topic was the structure of national government or economic policy. The presidential election unit could include a day for comparative reports by the three internationally experienced students on election processes in their host or home countries. When they studied the concept of leadership, perhaps Amin could tell about Nasser, Sadat, and Mubarak and Jacques could talk about DeGaulle and Mitterrand. "Why don't I know the name of any Swiss leader?" he asked himself.

An idea for projects which would enlarge the use of international resource persons and involve all students occurred to him. During the mock Congress which consumed the second trimester and focused on current issues, an outside project could require pairs of students to interview internationally experienced persons in the school or community in order to discover their perspectives on a current issue. The results of the interviews could be written up in short papers with titles such as "An Indonesian View of a Good Secondary Education."

The third trimester focused on local government, the judicial system, and international relations. Perhaps Celeste would be interested in doing research on Swiss cantons, Jacques on the influence of the Napoleonic Code in North America, and Amin on the fundamentals of Islamic law. Class might end with a mock U.S. Senate Foreign Relations Committee hearing on the future of American foreign policy, asking Celeste, Jacques, and Amin to be international witnesses.

APPENDIX 2: UTILIZATION OF INTERNATIONALLY EXPERIENCED (IE) PERSONS

AREA OF IMPACT OF INTERNATIONAL EXPERIENCE	STUDENTS	TEACHERS
SUBSTANTIVE KNOWLEDGE	Adopt a Student — elementary class adopts IE student	IE teacher develops culture kit
PERCEPTUAL UNDERSTANDING	World Issues Forum for IE and non-IE students on human rights	Teacher organizes panel of IE students to talk about environmental issues
PERSONAL GROWTH	IE and non-IE students participate in prejudice reduction workshop	IE teacher talks about confronting own prejudice
INTERPERSONAL CONNECTIONS	Class does pen pal exchange with school IE student attended in another country	Teacher organizes conversation partners for ESL students
CULTURAL MEDIATION	IE students act as buddies for new exchange students	IE teacher encourages IE student participation in class

APPENDIX 3: HOW TO BEGIN TO UTILIZE INTERNATIONALLY EXPERIENCED PERSONS IN A SCHOOL SYSTEM

The initiator:

  a teacher or principal in an individual school

  a social studies coordinator or foreign language or ESL coordinator

  a person in the central office

The initiating activity:

  a school or system resource inventory of students, teachers, parents, community people who have international experience

The organizing activities:

  a workshop for internationally experienced persons which requires something shared by each one and then brainstorming by small groups about how to utilize the experience

  a small committee (students, teachers, parents/community) to decide on one or several projects suggested in the brainstorming and to present those to the school, administrators, school board, as appropriate

The implementing activities:

  the same, enlarged, or different committee(s) to carry out the project, remembering not only to do the activity but to publicize and evaluate it

APPENDIX 4: EXCHANGE STUDENTS AS RESOURCES:
20 WAYS THEY CAN CONTRIBUTE

1. Be a language tutor or conversation partner for an American student.

2. Be a member of a panel of exchange students and exchange returnees talking about their cultures as part of a foreign language or social studies class unit.

3. Help initiate a pen pal and/or video exchange with the home or host school.

4. Organize an exhibit in the library focusing on "my" country.

5. Be part of an effort to recognize exchange student links over the years through a flag display or ongoing exhibit of one artifact from each country in the entrance to school.

6. Be part of library brown bag lunch series on Schooling Around the World.

7. Be part of school or system or regionwide day-long Forum for American and exchange students on an international issue such as the environment or hunger.

8. Be part of a school mock United Nations team participating in such an event sponsored by the Y or another organization.

9. Help organize an Exchange Fair at night to publicize exchange opportunities to students and their parents—and include international desserts!

10. Help organize International Dinner and Talent Show for community, perhaps working with foreign language classes and/or International Club.

11. Participate in morning announcements with questions on the Country of the Week—perhaps emphasizing geography and involving an appropriate prize.

12. Help make video to be used by others in school in which each person (representing the diversity of the school in terms of cultures of all kinds) talks about prejudice and ways to overcome it.

13. Write one of a series of articles entitled "Bringing a Global Perspective to _____ High" in school or local newspaper.

14. Help organize World Beat dance with music from around the world.

15. Demonstrate games, sports from home/host country in physical education classes.

16. Help construct graphs in math class showing comparative information about countries represented by exchange students and returnees and immigrants.

17. Help organize an art exhibit with a common theme, illustrated by people from different cultures.

18. Visit an elementary classroom, preferably at least twice, so children get to know visiting exchange student or returnee. Teach counting in

foreign language, a simple song, share some food, and be ready to answer lots of questions.

19. Visit a middle school classroom and talk about a day in the life of a 12-14 year old in the home or host country.

20. Be a constant resource in a social studies class.

APPENDIX 5: INTERNATIONALIZING A SECONDARY SOCIAL STUDIES METHODS CLASS

1. Use a global issue, such as world hunger, as focus of 10-day model unit to demonstrate . . .

   how to gather and make decisions about materials and teaching ideas

   how students gain knowledge, consider concepts, practice skills, and take action

2. Infuse a global perspective at other points in the course to demonstrate . . .

   use of research skills (Do research on linkage of aspect of community with world)

   use of literature in social studies (Read Mariama Ba's *So Long a Letter* about women in Senegal)

   use of learning centers (Set up learning centers on country where teacher has traveled or lived)

   use of media (Require subscription to *Christian Science Monitor* and have students develop strategies for dealing with current events)

3. Require 10 hours of cross-cultural experience as part of field experience which may include . . .

   being a conversation partner for an ESL student

   attending lectures, concerts, exhibits, movies with international or multicultural content

   and . . .

   writing a reflective paper on what was learned and how it applies to being a social studies teacher

APPENDIX 6: A HIERARCHY OF INTERCULTURAL EXPERIENCES FOR FUTURE TEACHERS

LEVEL	DESCRIPTION	EXAMPLES
INTERCULTURAL PARTICIPANT	Living and working in a culture not one's own	Student teaching in Latin America or in inner city U.S.A. by rural student
INTERCULTURAL FRIEND	Developing a one-to-one relationship with person of a culture not one's own	With international student or American of another culture
INTERCULTURAL OBSERVER	Observing a culture not one's own	Study tour in Europe or New Yorker in Appalachia or vice versa
INTERCULTURAL STUDENT	Reading about a culture not one's own	Course in Russian history or African-American literature
INTERCULTURAL DABBLER	Beginning to learn about a culture not one's own	Eating in a Greek restaurant or learning yoga or karate

APPENDIX 7: SYNERGY IN INTERNATIONAL EDUCATION

SCHOOL SYSTEM	HIGHER EDUCATION	COMMUNITY
INTERNATIONAL FAIR:		
Teachers bringing students, exhibits, performances	University providing place, international student clubs, teacher education students	Community groups offering tent, food, fashion show, bagpiper
WORLD AFFAIRS FORUM:		
IE students planning, leading discussion groups, initiating action project with teacher advice	University providing speaker on international topic, international and teacher education students as resources	Community group holding related essay contest, helping raise money for action project
STUDY TOUR:		
Teachers going on study tour and developing culture kits related to curriculum and organizing followup project such as pen pals	University providing orientation, credit, leader; teachers show kits to methods class	Community group providing contacts through Partners or Sister Cities and aiding followup project

Bibliography

Abe, H., and Wiseman, R. L. (1983). A cross-cultural confirmation of the dimensions of intercultural effectiveness. *International Journal of Intercultural Relations*. 7: 53-67.

Abrams, I. (1965). Why study abroad? (1991) *Occasional papers on international education exchange*. New York: Council on International Educational Exchange.

Adler, P. (1975). The transitional experience: an alternative view of culture shock. *Humanistic Psychology*. 15, 4: 13-23.

AFS (n.d.). Research identifies benefits for youth of intercultural homestays abroad. New York: AFS International/Intercultural Programs.

Agbayani, A. (1979). *Political definitions in research and educational progams that affect immigrant children in Hawaii*. National Association for Asian American and Pacific Education Conference, San Francisco.

Anderson, L. (1982). Why should American education be globalized: It's a nonsensical question. *Theory into Practice*. 21, 3: 155-161.

Ashabranner, B. (1968). From the Peace Corps, a new kind of teacher. *The National Elementary Principal*. April: 38-42.

Bachner, D. J., and Zeutschel, U. (1990). *Students of four decades: A research study of the influences of an international exchange experience on the lives of German and U.S. high school students*. Washington, D.C.: Youth for Understanding.

Baker, J. O. (1983). *A longitudinal study of the impact of study abroad on academic interests*. International Society for Educational, Cultural, and Scientific Exchanges, Cincinnati.

Barber, B. R. (1992). *An aristocracy of everyone: The politics of education and the future of America*. New York: Ballantine.

Bennett, C. I. (1990). *Comprehensive multicultural education: Theory and practice.* Boston: Allyn and Bacon.

Bjerstedt, A. (1962). Informational and non-informational determinants of nationality stereotypes. *Journal of Social Issues.* 18, 1: 24-29.

Blythe, R. (1969). *Akenfield.* New York: Dell.

Bochner, S., ed. (1981). *The mediating person: Bridges between cultures.* Boston: G. K. Hall.

Boswell, J. (1928). *Private papers, Boswell on the grand tour.* New York: McGraw Hill.

Brislin, R. W. (1981). Why live abroad?: Outcomes, human relations, and contributions to task effectiveness as key variables in educational exchanges. *East-West Culture Learning Institute Report.* Honolulu, Hawaii: East-West Center.

Brislin, R. W. (1983). The benefits of close intercultural relationships. In S. H. Irvine and J. W. Berry, eds., *Human assessment and cultural factors.* New York: Plenum Publishing.

Burn, B. (1982). The impact of the Fulbright experience on grantees from the United States. *ADFL Bulletin,* 14, 1: 39-43.

Butler, W. R. (1992). Beyond re-entry: the age of the emerging global international student and scholar. In D. McIntire and P. Willer, eds., *Working with international students and scholars on American campuses.* Washington, D.C.: National Association of Student Personnel Administrators.

Calvert, R. (1966). Two way street: Peace Corps and New York State teachers. *New York State Education.* October: 15-17.

Carlson, J. S., Burn, B. B., Useem, J., and Yachimowicz, D. (1991). *Study abroad: The experience of American undergraduates.* Westport, Conn.: Greenwood Press.

Carlson, J. S., Burn, B. B., Useem, and J. Yachimowicz, D. (1991). *Study abroad: The experience of American undergraduates in western Europe and the United States.* Occasional Paper 28. New York: Council on International Educational Exchange.

Case, R. (1991). *Key elements of a global perspective.* Occasional Paper. University of British Columbia: Centre for the Study of Curriculum and Instruction.

Christian Science Monitor (1960). Study abroad is necessity for college students. February 6.

Christian Science Monitor (1992). Immigrants flood New York City schools. May 18.

Cleveland, H. (1991). The open moment. *Esprimilo.* Youth for Understanding International Secretariat Newsletter. October: 3-6.

Coles, R. (1977). *Privileged ones,* Volume V of *Children of crisis.* Boston: Little, Brown.

Cook, B. W. (1992). *Eleanor Roosevelt,* Volume I. New York: Viking.

Cushner, K., McClelland, A., and Safford, P. (1992). *Human diversity in education: An integrative approach.* New York: McGraw-Hill.

Detweiler, R. A. (1984). *Youth for Understanding evaluation research: Cross-sectional study of 1977-1983 participants and longitudinal study of 1983 participants.* Washington, D.C.: Youth for Understanding.

Dumont, R. V., and Wax, M. L. (1976). Cherokee school society and the intercultural classroom. In J. I. Roberts and S. K. Akinsanya, eds., *Schooling in a cultural context.* New York: David McKay.

Ezekiel, R. S. (1969). The personal future and Peace Corps competence. *Journal of Personality and Social Psychology.* 2: 1-26.

Fuchs, L. H. (1967). *Those peculiar Americans: The Peace Corps and American national character.* New York: Meredith Press.

Gibson, M. A. (1983). *Home-school-community linkages: A study of educational opportunity for Punjabi youth.* South Asian American Educational Association, Stockton, Calif.

Gilliom, M. E. (n.d.). Study tour questionnaires. Unpublished. The Ohio State University.

Goodwin, C. D., and Nacht, M. (1988). *Abroad and Beyond: Patterns in American overseas education.* Cambridge: Cambridge University Press.

Grant, C. A. (1977). The mediator of culture: a teacher role revisited. *Journal of Research and Development in Education.* 11, 1: 85-101.

Grossman, D. L. (1992). Rationales for teaching about Japan: some reflections. In L. S. Wojtan and D. Spence, eds., *Internationalizing the U.S. classroom: Japan as a model.* ERIC Clearinghoue for Social Studies/Social Science Education and The National Clearinghouse of United States-Japan Studies.

Grove, C. L., and Hansel, B. (1982). *Impact of an AFS experience on American youth: Vol. I: The short program.* New York: AFS International/Intercultural Programs.

Grove, C. L., and Hansel, B. (1983). *Impact of an AFS experience on American youth: Vol. II: The year program.* New York: AFS International/Intercultural Programs.

Gullahorn, J. T., and Gullahorn, J. E. (1960). The role of the academic man as s cross-cultural mediator. *American Sociological Review.* 14: 414-417.

Hammer, M. R. (1987). Behavioral dimensions of intercultural effectiveness. *International Journal of Intercultural Relations.* II: 65-88.

Hansel, B. (1983). *The AFS impact study: Report of initial findings.* New York: AFS International/Intercultural Programs.

Hansel, B. (1984). *Literature review: Studies of the impact of a travel-abroad experience.* New York: AFS International/Intercultural Programs, Research Department 28.

Hansel, B. (1986). *The AFS impact study: Final report.* New York: AFS International/ Intercultural Programs, Research Department 33.

Hanvey, R. (1976). *An attainable global perspective.* New York: Global Perspectives in Education.

Hapgood, D., and Bennett, M. (1968). *Agents of change: A close look at the Peace Corps.* Boston: Little, Brown.

Harrington, C. C. (1975). *A psychological anthropologist's view of ethnicity and schooling.* New York: Institute for Urban and Minority Education, Teachers College, Columbia University.

Harris, J. G. (1973). A science of the South Pacific: Analysis of the character structure of the Peace Corps volunteer. *American Psychologist.* March: 232-47.

Hawes, F., and Kealey, D. (1979). *Canadians in development—An empirical study of adaptation and effectiveness on overseas assignment.* Ottawa: Canadian International Development Agency.

Henry, J. (1976). A cross-cultural outline of education. In J. S. Roberts and S. K.

Akinsanya, eds., *Educational patterns and cultural configurations*. New York: David McKay.

Higham, J. (1974). Integration vs. pluralism—another American dilemma. *The Center Magazine*. July/August.

Hoffman, J. E., and Zak, I. (1969). Interpersonal contact and attitude change in a cross-cultural situation. *The Journal of Social Psychology*. 78: 165-171.

James, H.E.O., and Tenen, C. (1951). Attitudes towards other peoples. *International Social Science Bulletin*. 3, 3: 553-561.

Johnson, D. (1972). *Levels of conceptualization in the teaching of Asian studies in the schools*. Columbus, Ohio: Service Center for Teachers of Asian Studies.

Kagiticibasi, C. (1978). Cross-national encounters: Turkish students in the United States. *International Journal of Intercultural Relations*. 2, 141-156.

Kauffmann, N. L. (1982). *The impact of study abroad on personality change*. Dissertation, Indiana University.

Kauffmann, N. L., Martin, J. N., and Weaver, H. D. (1992). *Students abroad: Strangers at home*. Yarmouth, Me.: Intercultural Press.

Kelman, H. C. (1962). Changing attitudes through international activities. *Journal of Social Issues*. 18: 68-87.

Kennan, G. F. (1989). *Sketches from a life*. New York: Pantheon Books.

Kennedy, G., ed. (1991). *From the center of the earth: Stories out of the Peace Corps*. Santa Monica, Calif.: Clover Park Press.

Kileff, C. (1975). The rebirth of a grandfather's spirit: Shumba's Two Worlds. *Human Organization*. 34, 2: 129-137.

Kim, Y. K. (1989). Intercultural adaptation. In M. F. Asante and W. B. Gudykunst, eds., *Handbook of international and intercultural communication*. Newbury Park, Calif.: Sage.

King, E. (1984). *Implications of Britain's mother tongue project for American education*. New Orleans, Louisiana: American Educational Research Association.

Kleinjans, E. (1974). *A question of ethics.*, Second annual shipboard international education conference, S. S. Universe Campus.

Kniep, W. M. (1986). Defining a global education by its content. *Social Education*. 50, 6: 437-446.

Knowles, J., Pietras, T., and Urick, T. (1970). Peace Corps veterans: an approach to urban education. *Contemporary Education*. October: 35-38.

Koester, J. (1985). *A profile of the U.S. student abroad*. New York: Council on International Educational Exchange.

Korten, D. C. (1990). *Getting to the 21st century: Voluntary action and the global agenda*. West Hartford, Conn.: Kumarian Press.

Kozoll, C. E. (1968). The ex-Peace Corps volunteer: asset or liability in teaching? *New York State Education*. April: 28-29.

Landrum, R. (1981). *The role of the Peace Corps in education in developing countries*. Washington, D.C.: Peace Corps Office of Planning and Evaluation.

Leed, E. J. (1991). *The mind of the traveler*. New York: Basic Books.

Leonard, E. W. (1964). Attitude change in a college program of foreign study and travel. *Educational Record*. 45, 2 173-181.

McDermott, R. P., and Gospedinoff, K. (1981). Social context for ethnic border and school failure. In H. T. Trueba, G. P. Guthries, and K. H. Au, eds., *Culture and bilingual classrooms: Studies in classroom ethnology*. Rawley, Mass.: Newbury House.

McKiernan, J. (1980). *An evaluation of the Consortium for Overseas Student Teaching and its effect on the expressed self-acceptance and acceptance of others of its participants.* Dissertation, University of Alabama.

Mahan, J. M., and Stachowski, L. L. (1985). Overseas student teaching: a model, important outcomes, recommendations. *International Education.* 15, 1: 9-28.

Martin, J. N. (1986). Communication in the intercultural reentry: student sojourners' perceptions of change in reentry relationship. *International Journal of Intercultural Relations.* 10: 1-22.

Mead, W. E. (1914). *The grand tour in the eighteenth century.* Boston: Houghton Mifflin.

Merryfield, M. M. (1991). Preparing American secondary social studies teachers to teach with a global perspective: a status report. *Journal of Teacher Education.* January–February, 42, 1: 11-20.

Miller, J. (1983). *Many voices: Bilingualism, culture, and education.* London, Boston: Routledge and Kegan Paul.

Milman, J. (1984). *A case study of a bilingual American school in Mexico.* Dissertation, University of Kentucky.

Moore, G. A. (1976). Realities of the urban classroom. In J. I. Roberts and S. K. Akinsanya, eds., *Schooling in the cultural context.* New York: David McKay.

Mukai, G. (1992). Anatomy of a curriculum development project. In L. S. Wojtan and D. Spence, eds., *Internationalizing the U.S. classroom: Japan as a model.* Boulder, Colorado: ERIC Clearinghouse for Social Studies/Social Science Education and The National Clearinghouse for United States-Japan Studies.

Naisbitt, J. (1982). *Megatrends.* New York: Warner.

Nash, D. (1976). The consequences of a year of study abroad. *Journal of Higher Education.* 47: 191-203.

Ogbu, J. U. (1974). *The next generation: An ethnography of education in an urban neighborhood.* New York: Academic Press.

Ogbu, J. U. (1978). *Minority education and caste: The American system in cross-cultural perspective.* New York: Academic Press.

Patrick, J. J. (1986). Immigration in the curriculum. *Social Education.* 50, 3: 172-175.

Peskin, A. (1991). *The color of strangers, the color of friends: The play of ethnicity in school and community.* Chicago: University of Chicago Press.

Ping, C. J. (1982). International education at Ohio University: the search for international community and education for interdependence. Unpublished paper.

Rambo, B. (1992). Travelers. *The Global Nomad Quarterly.* I, 1: 6.

Reed, I. (1988). America: the multinational society. In R. Simonson and S. Walker, eds., *Multicultural Literacy: Opening the American mind.* St. Paul, Minn.: Graywolf Press.

Report of the Study Commission on Global Education (1987). *The United States prepares for its future: Global perspectives in education.* New York: Global Perspectives in Education.

Rice, G. T. (1981). *Twenty years of Peace Corps.* Washington, D.C.: Peace Corps.

Schaetti, B. (1992). Using who we are: global nomads in multicultural organizations. *The Global Nomad Quarterly.* I, 1: 3-4.

Schama, S. (1989). *Citizens: A chronicle of the French Revolution.* New York: Alfred A. Knopf.

Sell, D. (1983). Research on attitude change in U.S. students who participate in foreign study experiences: Past findings and suggestions for future re-search. *International Journal of Intercultural Relations*. 7: 131-147.

Sharma, M. P., and Jung, L. B. (1986). How cross-cultural participation affects the international attitudes of U.S. students. *International Journal of Intercultural Relations*. 10: 377-387.

Smith, C. D. (1991). *The absentee American: Repatriates' perspectives on America and its place in the contemporary world*. Westport, Conn.: Praeger.

Smith, H. P. (1954). Do intercultural experiences affect attitudes? *Journal of Abnormal and Social Psychology*. 51, 3: 469-477.

Smith, H. P. (1957). The effects of intercultural experience: a follow-up investigation. *Journal of Abnormal and Social Psychology*. 54, 2: 266-269.

Smith, M. B. (1966). Explorations in competence: a study of Peace Corps teachers in Ghana. *American Psychologist*. June: 555-556.

Speakman, C. E. (1966). *International exchange in education*. New York: Center for Applied Research in Education.

Spindler, G., ed. (1982). *Doing the ethnography of schooling: Educational anthropology in action*. New York: Holt, Rinehart and Winston.

Stewart, R.A.C. (1976). Personality change: the effects on New Zealand adolescents of a scholarship exchange year in the U.S.A. *Adolescence in New Zealand*. Auckland and London: Heinemann.

Stitsworth, M. H. (1988). The relationship between previous foreign language study and personality change in youth exchange participants. *Foreign Language Annuals*. 21, 2: 131-137.

Stohl, C. (1986). The A.M.I.G.O. project. *International Journal of Intercultural Relations*. 10: 151-177.

Stonequist, E. V. (1937). *The marginal man*. New York: Charles Scribner's Sons.

Sussman, N. M. (1986). Reentry research and training: methods and implications. *International Journal of Intercultural Relations*. 10: 235-254.

Takaki, R. (1989). *Strangers from a different shore: A history of Asian Americans*. New York: Penguin.

Taylor, H. (1969). *The world as teacher*. New York: Doubleday.

Thomlison, T. D. (1991). Effects of a study-abroad program on university students: toward a predictive theory of intercultural contact. Paper presented at Intercultural Communication Conference, Miami.

Thorpe, S. (1988). The impact of high school social studies teachers' backgrounds and organizational environments on the implementation of global education curricula. Paper presented at annual meeting of National Council for the Social Studies, Orlando.

Time. May 11, 1992, cover.

Tuch, H. N. (1988). *Arthur Burns and the successor generation: Selected writings of and about Arthur Burns*. Lanham, Md.: University Press of America.

Tyack, D. B. (1967). *Turning points in American educational history*. Blaisdell.

Tye, B. B., and Tye, K. A. (1992). *Global education: A study of school change*. Albany, N.Y.: State University of New York Press.

Tye, K. A., ed. (1990). *Global education: From thought to action*. 1991 Yearbook. Alexandria, Va.: Association for Supervision and Curriculum Development.

Uehara, A. (1986). The nature of American student reentry adjustment and perceptions of the sojourn experience. *International Journal of Intercultural Relations*. 10: 415-438.

Vall, N. G., and Tennison, J. M. (1991-92). International student teaching: stimulus for developing reflective teachers. *Action in teacher education*, 13, 4: 30-36.

Van de Water, J. (1986). Foreign students: untapped resource. *Christian Science Monitor.* November 17: B4.

Volunteer (1971). Peace Corps. Vol. 5-6. Summer.

Warren, P. B. (1967). The Peace Corps returnee—teacher? *Phi Delta Kappan.* June: 520-522.

Washington, B. (1964). *Cardozo project in urban teaching, a pilot project in curriculum development utilizing returned Peace Corps volunteers in an urban high school.* Interim report. Washington, D.C.: District of Columbia Schools.

Weiss, B. J., ed. (1982). *American education and the European immigrant: 1840-1940.* Urbana: University of Illinois Press.

West, C. (1992). Learning to talk of race. *The New York Times Magazine*, August 2: 24-26.

Wieber, D. (1982). *Assessment of global knowledge of K–12 teachers in an American-sponsored overseas school.* Doctoral dissertation, Michigan State University.

Wilson, A. H. (1979). Multicultural experiences, global perspective and teacher education. *The Teacher Educator.* 15, 2: 29-33.

Wilson, A. H. (1982). Cross-cultural experiential learning for teachers. *Theory into Practice.* 21, 3: 184-192.

Wilson, A. H. (1983). A case study of two teachers with cross-cultural experience: they know more. *Educational Research Quarterly.* 8, I: 78-85.

Wilson, A. H. (1984). Teachers as short-term sojourners: opening windows on the world. *The Social Studies.* 75, 4: 184-192.

Wilson, A. H. (1985). Returned exchange students: becoming mediating persons. *International Journal of Intercultural Relations.* 9: 285-305.

Wilson, A. H. (1986a). The immigrant student challenge. *Social Education.* 50, 3: 189-193.

Wilson, A. H. (1986b). Returned Peace Corps volunteers who teach social studies. *The Social Studies.* 77, 3: 100-107.

Wilson, A. H. (1991). The impact of international experience: research and questions. Paper presented at NAFSA: Association of International Educators regional meeting, Toledo.

Wilson, A. H. (1992). *International student speaker programs: "someone from another world."* NAFSA Working Paper #35. Washington, D.C.: NAFSA: Association of International Educators.

Wilson, A. H. (1993). Conversation partners: gaining a global perspective through cross-cultural experiences. *Theory into Practice.* 32: 1, 21-26.

Wilson, A. H. (n.d.). Reentry of study abroad students. Unpublished research.

Wilson, J. A. (1966). Reverse culture shock in Cleveland. *Peace Corps Volunteer.* May: 20-21.

Winslow, E. A. (1977). A survey of returned Peace Corps volunteers. Peace Corps.

Zulich, J. (1989). Hawaii's school system is one of a kind. *Phi Delta Kappan.* 70, 7: 546-549.

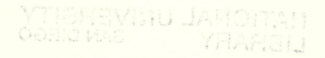

Index

About the Author

ANGENE HOPKINS WILSON is a Professor in the Department of Curriculum and Instruction at the University of Kentucky, and Associate Director of its Office of International Affairs. She was a Peace Corps volunteer teacher in the 1960s, and a teacher educator in West Africa and the South Pacific. Wilson has written and spoken extensively about internationalization of university campuses.